THE BEST LAST THING
TO DO

P. J. HARVEY

Mandurang Press

PO Box 2063, Bendigo DC, Victoria 3554, Australia

First published by Mandurang Press 2020

Book design by Vellum

Book cover by Louisa West

Printed and bound by Ingram

ISBN: 978-0-6484776-6-2 (paperback)

ISBN: 978-0-6484776-5-5 (ebook)

A catalogue record for this book is available from the National Library of Australia

For Tony and Tom

1

BULL

It's the first day of January, dry as old bones, hotter than Grace Fountain in her shorts and tank top, and Kendo's making us play football on the dead school oval.

'Bull!'

The ball heads towards me like a nuclear bomb and hits me in the stomach. I clutch at my guts and accidentally hold the ball as well.

'Free kick!' Charlie shouts but I can see Kendo shake his head so that his blond sweaty hair spins. 'Play on!'

Whatever. I turn towards the nearest goal posts and drop the ball on my bare foot. It zings off my toes, goes somewhere it shouldn't, and Lewis comes from nowhere to sweep it up. I watch in relief as play takes it away from me, and lean on my thighs to catch my breath. Through the sweat pouring down my face, I see Kendo tackle Lewis so they fall heavily on the dirt. Charlie snatches the ball and shoots it lazily through the centre posts.

I walk slowly over to Lew who's still on the ground. Kendo is running after the ball like a crazed man, his body muscled and shiny in the hard light. I sit down on the neglected oval, tug my shirt over my vast stomach, watch Charlie – a whole head shorter than anyone on the field - and Kendo fight over the pigskin, and shake my head. 'I can't believe we're friends with those idiots.'

Lewis is holding onto his foot. 'I can't believe we're playing football instead of being at the pool.' He rubs his toe.

'What's the matter?'

'Took the skin off.' He holds his foot up for me to see. His toe has been skinned so that the top layer of skin is folded onto itself. Blood runs back to his ankle.

'You all right?'

'It'll be fine.' Lewis wipes at his toe with his hand, and then cleans his hand on my T-shirt.

'Hey! Watch it, this is Kurt.'

Lewis pretends to be surprised and leans closer to the faded head on my shirt front. 'You got any other T-shirts than ones with dead guys on them?'

I push him away. 'What do you think? Anyway, you gave me this last birthday, wanker.'

Charlie and Kendo run over. Charlie slams the ball next to Lewis and sits down, pulling Kendo with him. For a moment we roast together in the sun, Kendo thumping the ball to make it bounce, Charlie stretched out on his back, Lewis trying not to let us see how much pain he's in.

'I need a drink,' I say finally, standing up and moving towards the taps.

No one follows me as I go under the shade of the senior wing building and drink the warm water down greedily. I stick my head under as far as I can and rub at my hair until I'm drenched. Even so, I'm nearly dry again by the time I walk back to the others. The sky growls, though. Another summer storm is brewing. I think about going home before it rains to do some serious work on a piece I just downloaded from the internet. An old one but new to me, it has tricky chord changes and a bit of fast finger work that reminds me that I need a new plectrum for a sharper sound-

'Bull!'

'What?'

'You deaf?' Kendo stands up and knocks at the side of my head. 'Can't have a deaf musician. Charlie said. We're going to get burgers.'

'Beethoven,' I say.

'*What?*'

'Beethoven was deaf.'

Kendo rolls his eyes and gives me a kind pat on the back with his iron fist that nearly knocks me over. 'He was also crazy. Burgers!'

'Not burgers! Pizza.'

'Actually, yeah. Bull and I, we don't like burgers because we make too many.'

'Pizza, then. Come on.' Charlie rolls himself upright, grabs at Lewis to haul him up too, and we head to town. 'Anything. Before we fade away.'

I point to my stomach. 'Quick. I really am fading away.'

They laugh and I grin. We must look ridiculous together – skinny Lewis, enormous me, muscly Kendo and hairy Charlie. Who'd believe we were all sixteen?

We walk slowly towards the pizza shop. The sky gradually clouds over but it doesn't get any cooler. If anything, it's worse. We're in an oven with the door shut. Kendo's still bouncing the ball, Lewis is talking to Charlie about his boring Christmas day, so I take the lead.

Carefully, so no one notices, I go the slightly long way around to avoid the park. We get to the shop to find that the air-conditioner has broken and the main chef has fainted in the heat so we end up sitting in the café next door (which might not be our normal habitat but has air-conditioning), ordering iced coffees and hot chips.

Lewis flicks idly through a newspaper that's been left on the table while we wait. Kendo's texting, Charlie's counting out his five cent pieces to see if he's got enough for a vanilla slice, when Lewis slides the paper across to me. 'Hey, isn't that Janet's house?'

I look before I can stop myself. The real estate pages are in front of me, neat squares of pictures and lies, trying to entice buyers. Some of them are slashed with 'SOLD.' A stupid thing to do, I think, showing pictures of houses already sold in the 'For Sale' section. I follow Lewis' tapping finger until I see what he means. My Aunt Janet's house has bold white letters across it. SOLD.

Your house has sold, Josh.

Your mum is leaving.

Your bed and wardrobe and posters and bike will go as well.

'Bull, you right?' Lewis speaks quietly but Kendo looks up and Charlie stops counting.

'Yeah, yeah. I just didn't know. I didn't know…'

Luckily, the drinks arrive. Lewis shuts the paper, reaches across to put it on another table, and takes a fat chip out of Kendo's bowl.

'Hey!'

'What?'

Kendo reaches over to Lewis and thumps him. 'Don't touch the chips!'

Charlie takes one as well and gets a battering of punches that makes him growl, 'Okay, okay, sorry, sorry, have your bloody chips then.'

Among my friends and their stupid mucking around, I slowly return to normal.

But when we've eaten and get up to leave, I realize that I don't feel completely normal. I do know that all I want to do is to get home and pick up my guitar and shut the bedroom door and play until my fingers bleed, just like you did that time, Josh. That first mad time, when you played for six hours straight and the strings of your Yamaha were smeared red. It would be different for me, though. You played because you were driven. I play because music is in my blood.

We peel off our separate ways, planning to go swimming the next day and every next day of the holidays if it stays hot and doesn't rain too much.

'Happy New Year,' says Lewis as I leave him.

'Yeah.' I watch him briefly before turning away.

A New Year. It should be the start of something new. For a moment I forget what that could be. Then I remember.

A New Year without you.

2
———

LEWIS

My toe is throbbing from where I hit the dust. I try
to ignore it, concentrating instead on how dark the
room is except for the single creamy light trained on my
Keally-branded sketchpad. This is exactly how I need it to
be able to draw. If Mum comes in, she wrenches the
curtains open and mutters, 'You're going to ruin your eyes.'

'But I have a desk lamp,' I always protest. 'It's not like
I've just got the stub of a candle.'

'Yes, well, I don't know,' she'll mutter darkly and leave.

Yes, well, I *do* know. I'd like to feel sorry for Mum,
having to put up with me and the way things are, but she
always thinks she's right. How can you feel sorry for a
person like that?

I try to use a different pencil every day. I don't like
seeing my favourites wear down quicker than the rest. If
anyone had asked, I'd say that I match the colour of the
pencil to my mood but really that's bullshit. I'm going on
length here. Mum gave me this box of *100 Artist's Colours*
when I first got sick, when she didn't know what was wrong
with me and was trying anything to make me better. Cure

by pencil. It didn't work, of course, but I've still got the box. I've never told Mum how much I like it. I like the way the pencils feel under my fingers when I run my hand over them, I like the way they smell. But most of all I like the way, when I first open the box, I have something new in front of me. A whole box full of potential drawings.

Thanks, Mum. Really.

Today I'm using lime. Colour of the fruit and three quarters of the way on the colour chart between yellow and green, tending on the yellow side. So the experts say. I like it because limes stopped sailors getting scurvy and that's a pretty amazing thing for a sour little green ball.

The pencil makes a light scratching noise across the heavy paper. I'm drawing quickly, hurrying to catch the moment while I've got it happening. The week went so fast. Normally I can keep up with things but the start of school is always a difficult time.

'There's a bit of readjustment', The Judge would say. 'A bit of change to the routine. You'll get used to it again, Lewis Pascoe.'

Here's the week as it unrolled:

Monday started with a poor schoolboy who knows it's the end of the holidays. He wears his too-small uniform and carries a bag full of shiny books. The bag is weighing him down. He starts the week by walking towards school.

By Tuesday, he's got to the corner and some of the books have fallen out. His back is straighter, the load's lighter but he tugs at his shirt to stop it riding up his back.

By Wednesday he can see the school building, the huge new gym that celebrates all that is good at the school – sport, sport and a bit more sport. His bag is very light as most of the books have gone but he also realizes that he's forgotten his PE uniform – again.

By Thursday – the day it all begins – he's got to the

school gate. His bag's gone, thrown into the bushes. There're his mates sitting on the fence waiting. Their shirts are too small as well. Ah! The boy smiles because he gets the reason he's really at school. It's those fugly friends of his. But then one says, 'How ya feeling?'

My pencil tip snaps. I wish they wouldn't ask me those sorts of things. They don't ask their other friends. To them, they'd say, 'How ya going?' Me? They've got to check out if I'm going to be normal or not that day.

'How ya feeling, Lewis?'

'Going to freak out on us today, Lewis?'

I've lost my eraser in the doona so I wipe at the words with my finger, smudging them into a blob of dirty green and making the other kids shut up. I feel a bit light. Sort of not-really-there. My toe hurts. I rub it and get ooze on my finger. I wipe the gunk on my shorts.

Friday. The boy is fine because he can smell the weekend. He leaves school behind him and makes it home in superman-red time. He shuts the door to his bedroom and takes out his pencil. The boy smiles, relaxes, lets it all flow. The week's finished. He wasn't sick. He made it.

I put down my pencil but almost straight away pick it up again. Now I've got that down I can start a new story. I know that some people keep diaries to make sense of what happens in their life – not anyone I know, they'd rather eat ten live spiders than confess something like that. I don't see my sketchbook as a diary, though. I just draw things. I've got eight other sketchbooks, all full of pictures, just the things that happen every day. No big deal.

There's a knock at the door.

'Lewis?'

'Yes, it's open.'

Mum comes in, frowns at the darkened room so I save

her the hassle and pull open the curtain. She nods her approval. 'Everything okay?'

That's a code sentence for *howareyoufeeling* but it's different when Mum says it. Mums are meant to ask things like that, not that she'd ever come out and say it properly unless she was really worried. We have a few codes between us, Mum and me. 'Not bad,' I say, meaning *I'mnotfantasticbutI'llbegood*. She nods again and leaves, the door staying ajar like she meant it to.

I can hear Dad in the lounge. He coughs and rustles the TV guide. Ten minutes tops and he'll be asleep in his chair, worn out from a hard day at the office. Mum will finish up whatever she does to keep her family going and then she'll finally sit down to read the paper. She won't fall asleep. She doesn't go to bed until everyone else has. At least now she can sleep through the whole night.

It wasn't always like that. In those early years I was usually bad about two o'clock in the morning and she had to come and check me. 'Come and eat something, Lewis.' I ate, she watched. Then they put me on a new type of insulin. We can both sleep now. Such a stupid thing but God, it makes a difference. I hadn't realized I loved sleep so much.

The pencil falls out of my hand and I reach down to pick it up. I'm sick of my story. I turn to a new page, and lightly sketch my best friend's face. I put Bull in a whirlwind, make him spin around and around. He's like a willy-willy in the summer, kicking up dust and debris. I suppose he can't help it but it worries me sometimes.

'...and that's the end of the news,' the TV says. I shut the sketchbook. Out in the lounge, as I guessed, Dad's asleep, Mum's in her chair reading the paper. I raise my eyebrows at her and she nods, so I gently tug the remote from Dad's hand and change the channel. His lips tighten but his eyes stay shut. I turn down the volume a bit before stretching out on the couch to watch some TV unreality show about bad kids. Mum's hand settles on my head for a moment and then it's gone. She turns the page on the paper but I still feel where her hand rested. Family in harmony, I can relax.

3

BULL

'Go on, no way! It's *not* out!'

I look up from where I sit on the couch checking guitar strings. Dad is watching the cricket on the 24 hour sports channel. He's been doing it for days, spending his hard-earned holidays as a coach potato. Mugs and beer cans stack up on the coffee table beside him.

'What happened, Dad?'

Dad points at the telly with his new can and gives it a shake. 'Will, that umpire needs glasses.' The video replay comes on and it's clear that Dad is the one who needs glasses. I chuckle. 'Are they sure?' Dad grumbles under his breath. 'Looked out to me.'

Mum walks past, bristling as she glares at the pile of stuff next to Dad. No way is she going to pick up his rubbish, but it nearly kills her to see the mess. I think if I were her I'd just pick it up now. 'Grown man,' I hear her mutter in the kitchen. 'Pick up his own mugs.'

Liar. She knows she's going to do it as soon as he leaves the lounge room.

Save the angst, you'd say, *do it now.* 'Mum,' I almost say to her, 'Dad really doesn't care if he's surrounded by rubbish'. He steps over the *Telford Guardian* spread out on the carpet, chucks the three remotes on the couch, peels off his tank top and drops it on the chair next to his. When he balances his beer glass on top of Great-Grandma's piano that came out from England on a boat, even *I* cringe. Dad hasn't got a nasty bone in his body, wouldn't upset a fly. He just doesn't *get it* when it comes to housework. Mum takes on his share, cleaning this house to a shining home-beauty sparkle that makes my friends too nervous to visit.

The phone rings. El is quick to answer it. 'Hello, Ella speaking,' she says in her high, polite, thirteen year old girly voice. She pauses, listening just long enough for her face to drop and her shoulders to sag, and I know the call's not for her. 'He's here,' she says and passes it to me.

I still think every phone call I get is gonna be you. I remember in time. 'Yeah?'

'Bull. I can't do my maths.'

It's Lewis. He can never do his maths. 'No good asking me. I missed maths. Had a music lesson.'

He groans. 'What good are you?'

In the background I can hear his mum. 'The lawns, Ian. You need to mow the lawns. Today, Ian,' she's telling his dad. Lewis's mum is like that. When she asks, you do. We call her The Judge because her word is the law at the Pascoes.' I hear Lewis shut his bedroom door and The Judge's voice disappears.

Lewis sighs. 'Well, I can't do any more maths then.' Not a hint of sadness in his voice. 'What're you up to?'

'Not much. Too hot.' The temperature is pushing 38. 'Why you doing homework, anyway? We've only had two days of school.'

'I'm on a mission. Dad says he'll give me fifty dollars for every A I get.'

'Fifty bucks! What did your mum say about that?'

'What, you reckon she knows? No way. This is between me and Dad.'

I grunt. 'I think your dad's in front.' It'll be a lottery win if Lewis gets even one A. He's pretty smart but he's not interested in anything but drawing. I have an idea to bring him back to reality. 'Is your toe all right?' I ask.

Ten seconds pass while Lew checks out his pus-filled sore. 'Yes.'

'Then come swimming,' I say.

He pauses for a nanosecond. 'Right.'

It's when I'm getting changed that one of those moments sweeps over me. Last summer, we were at the pool all the time.

'Hey, Josh, want to go to the pool?'

'Yep.'

Even when Bonnie came into the picture.

'Hey, Josh, want to go the pool?'

'Yep. I'll just ring Bonnie.'

Bonnie. Can't tell you how much I hate her now.

I've got one leg in my boardies and I feel the cloud wrap around me. I'm suddenly so tired I've got to sit down on the bed. It's like plunging into a cold well, walls all around me, dark and scary. I have to wait it out - I know this - and so I do. My phone pings and I put my other leg groggily into my shorts before replying. *Late. Puncture.* It takes another five minutes to get the energy to walk out the door.

'Going for a swim, William?' says Mum. She's wiping the kitchen bench down, smooth-stroking the top, around and around and around.

'That okay? I'll be back by dinner.'

She nods. 'Fine. Off you go.'

El hears. 'Can I come, too?' Then Sofie starts. 'Can I come, can I come?'

We used to take them to the pool together but I don't want to handle them on my own. I look to Mum, waiting to see if Sofie's whining has triggered one of her moods. She's okay, though, and is on my side – what a surprise. 'No, girls. Not today. William's going with a friend.' The bench top cops another round of wiping.

'A *girl*friend,' El starts.

I glare, think of the dark and beautiful Grace, and have to duck my head to stop my face giving me away. 'Yeah, right,' I say. 'See ya.'

It takes ten minutes to ride to the pool, three minutes to ride home. We live at the bottom of the hill and the pool is at the top. We got it right when we moved here from Adelaide. I get stinking hot riding up the hill and it's all I can do to wave my season ticket at the guy on the gate before I crash into the cold blue water at the deep end. On the way home, I coast down and can make it into the drive without even touching the pedals. Lewis lives on the other side so he can do the same thing. When we want to go to each other's house, though, the long low hill is between us. In summer, we usually meet at the pool.

'Hey, Bull, over here!' Charlie's yelling at me.

Most of the South Telford Secondary mob is already here: Jules, Kendo and Charlie. And Grace. They're lying under the shade sails, along with everyone else, but have put up a barrier of bags. I try not to look at Grace but see straight away that she's given herself a Texta tattoo of a skull on her right calf.

Lewis is just pulling himself out of the water so I dump my stuff with the others and keep walking. He tries to grab my ankles but he's not quick enough and I jump over him into the numbing bedrock cold of the Telford Public Pool.

I close my eyes and let myself sink until my ears start singing. I like the quiet of underwater. I like the aloneness.

But I can't breathe and my lungs start to hurt. I don't want to end up like you, so I pull myself up and gasp in some air. Lewis dunks me. I hit him in the guts. We end up drinking the pool water, gagging on the chlorine like little kids, and fight our way to the edge to rest.

The South mob is being cool and they don't like us dripping over them as we get our towels. Jules squeals 'Get away!' and it makes me grind my teeth. She's hot to look at but when she does that it reminds me of seven year old Sofie. Jules turned sixteen last October – she had the whole home class to her party. Except me. I was still out of it then.

Still out of it.

'Bull,' yells Charlie. 'While you're up, get me some chips.' He throws coins and I catch them. Never miss any money chucked at me.

'Get your own, you lazy mongrel.' But I'm suddenly starving and need a trip to the canteen myself. I buy a pie, chips and two drinks. As I hand over my money, I hear they're playing my number 58. I go back to my friends. Throw the chips at Charlie. Throw a drink to Lewis. Stuff my face with the rest.

'Hey,' says Kendo, his buff body tanned and gleaming, 'there's Bonnie.'

Grace gives me a look from under her dark, damp curls. I hold her stare but let go first. The pie rises in my throat and I swallow it down hard.

Bonnie wanders over, water drops sparkling on her skin, pauses next to Jules, ignores me, and says, 'Anyone going to Jordan's tonight?'

Kendo hoots and Charlie grins. 'Only me,' says Grace lazily.

Bonnie sits down side-on to me but I lie face down on my towel, turn my head away from her and keep my eyes on Grace. 'You have to be there,' says Bonnie to Grace.

'I don't have to. But he is my aunty's step-son, sort of my cousin.'

I flinch. I hope no-one sees.

'He's not related to you too, is he, Bon?' Kendo says. I can hear the grin in his voice.

'Not yet,' Charlie says through a mouthful of chips.

'Bonnie and Jordan, match of the month,' says Kendo.

'Shut up,' Grace says.

'Yeah, Kendo, shut up.' Jules can only repeat what someone else has said.

'Don't tell him to shut up, shut up yourself.' Charlie grins at Grace.

In reply, she squeezes out her wet hair so that pool water drips on his bare back.

I don't want to see Grace play with Charlie and I definitely don't want to join in teasing Bonnie. I close my eyes.

I don't understand how quickly everything went back to normal. Normal for everyone but me. Maybe I do understand Jules, Grace, Charlie and Kendo – they didn't really have anything to do with you. But Bonnie. I don't understand Bonnie. How could she? I feel anger close my throat. How *could* she?

'Come on, Hereford.' Lewis grabs my hair and yanks me up. I swat him away. 'It's too hot. Let's go in again.'

For sure. Anything to get away from *her*. I beat him to the water and plunge in again. He swims right past me and climbs out the other side to get to the diving pool. I follow. We bomb and belly-whack and somersault off the three metre until Lewis pulls out. I keep going, fuelled by that rage that seems to fill me whenever I think of you and Bonnie, and then Bonnie and Jordan. I run up the ladder, throw myself into the water, get out of the pool and do it all again. Soon, there's no one else in the queue and I get into a rhythm. I climb out, run up the ladder, jump, smash into the water. I try to imagine it as a slow succession of notes in a minor chord – the root, minor third, a fifth, minor seventh. My ears start to ring. On the next seventh, I notice that Charlie and Kendo have joined Lewis. They're standing watching me, their arms folded.

'That's enough, Bull,' says Lewis.

I run past him and do another third, fifth and seventh.

Lewis is at the pool edge.

'Enough,' he says, grabbing me hard by the arm and walking us back to our towels.

Charlie and Kendo have gone. The girls have gone. Grace gone is like the sun clouding over. I sit in the shade, shivering now with cold and a skin-tingling exhaustion. I wonder how long I've been climbing and diving. Lewis sits next to me. The sun is getting lower. The glare hits the water and ricochets into my eyes.

'I wish you wouldn't do that,' Lewis says, pulling at the blades of grass next to him.

'What?'

'That.' Lewis nods toward the diving pool. I say nothing, feel nothing. 'And you shouldn't keep being so shitty to Bonnie.'

'I could be worse,' I say.

'You need to start talking to her again.'

Hey, Josh, did you hear that? My best friend wants me to talk to your old girlfriend. As if. I feel the rage flicker at my soul, so I turn away from Lewis and look at the clock under the veranda. 'God, I'd better go.' I stand up. 'Mum'll kill me if I'm not back in time for Saturday night chops.' The sky is getting dark. I can see lightning and there's that strange smell that comes with dangerous thunderstorms.

Lewis stands up as well. He staggers once. I look at him, glance down at his maggoty toe. 'You all right?'

'Yes.' He drapes his towel around his neck, doesn't say anything else.

We unchain our bikes, say goodbye, and ride off in opposite directions, each with those secrets we aren't sharing with anyone else.

———

'WILLIAM,' says Mum as I make it into the kitchen, 'you are late. Ella has done your jobs.'

That'll make up for the times that I've done hers, I almost say. 'Sorry, Mum.'

Mum humphs. She does that a lot. She hands me two plates to take to the table and I pass them to Dad and Sofie. We sit and eat in silence. Despite the pie, I'm starving. The pool does that. *You used to eat half a loaf of ham sandwiches after we went swimming. One time you ate a whole loaf.* I finish before anyone else but have to sit and wait. The thunder rumbles outside, making the house shake. I drum my fingers on the table, the intro riff from *Thunderstruck* playing in my head.

Mum finishes, puts her knife and fork together on the plate, spends a bit of time getting them straight. She humphs again. 'Janet has asked whether we can go and help her Monday.'

I don't say anything. The drumming stops. I look down at my fingers in surprise.

'What's she got left to do?' says Dad, picking his teeth with the end of his fork.

'She's got a moving company packing for her but there're some bits and pieces she wants to do first.

Cleaning up. Packing the special things.' She glances at me, looks down at her knife, straightens it a millimetre.

'Yeah, we can help.' Dad stretches. 'I'll be back at work and the cricket's not on until later.'

'I'm busy,' I say.

'William,' says Mum.

Thunder rumbles louder.

'Janet especially wants you to come along, Will.'

'I'll go,' says El, the angel of the family. No one takes any notice.

'I'm busy,' I say again a bit louder, a bit more desperately.

'We'll all go,' says Dad, unexpectedly firm. 'We won't see her as often when she moves. She's family. We need to help her.'

'Sorry, but I can't do it.' I stand up without excusing myself – a cardinal sin with Mum – and take my plate to the sink. It wobbles in my hand but I get it there. Behind me I can hear Sofie say, 'Will's gone without asking.' I leave my family at the table and go into my room.

My room has a double bed and wardrobe that were my grandpa's before he went into a home. They're made from a dark, polished wood. I used to hate them, hate the fact that they held Grandpa's things, that the bed was hollowed to the shape of his skinny old-man body. Dad got me a new mattress. I covered the wardrobe with posters of Brainchild. Before too long, they were mine. That's what happens when you have a room of your own – you make it yours.

That's the reason I haven't been into your bedroom. It's still yours. It'll smell like your sports deodorant. Your posters are still on the walls. I know Aunt Janet hasn't changed the sheets since you left. You're still there among the shoes and the car mags and the crooked mirror on the wall that's cracked in one corner from where you threw a football at me and I didn't – couldn't – catch it. I can't go to your home, I can't go into your bedroom because I will see that **you're not there anymore.**

The rain starts, hard and loud, lashing at the house. Aunt Janet will just have to pack up without me.

GOD, I'd thought the nightmares had stopped.

This time, I'm chasing you around the streets of Telford. I'm too big to run fast but you only just keep in front of me. *Catch me, Bull! See if you can catch me!* We run around all the places we used to hang out – Richter's Milkbar, the old playground next to the kindergarten, the outer edge of the skate park. They flash past us, then again as we run in circles. On the third or fourth go, I start to scream at you. *Josh! Stop!* My voice is weird and more like Sofie's than mine. *Stop! Josh!*

So we're running and I'm screaming *Josh! Stop!* and it's gone on and on for ages when suddenly you turn around. We aren't where we were. We're at the place you died and you start chasing me. *Catch me, Bull!* This time I'm just screaming, screaming, because you look like you did that day, chalky white face smeared with scarlet blood.

I wake panting. I hope I haven't been yelling out or Mum will be on the phone to Mr Peterson before I can get out of bed to stop her. Mr Peterson speaks in a calm voice that sometimes makes me think that he's not listening although he knows just what to say and when to say it. But I don't need Mr Peterson or the Bereavement Centre or the pastoral care worker from school.

I just need you, Josh, and you left me.
You prick.

4

LEWIS

Pale ultramarine – no. Royal blue – no. Kingfisher?

It's difficult to capture the colours of the pool. There's not a sole pencil that does it. Last summer I used a shadow of teal and overlaid it with mid ultramarine – that seemed to work then. Not this year, though. Up until this summer we'd had ten years of drought and the water in the pool was bleached from a constant supply of chemicals to keep it fresh. This year it's done nothing but rain. Now the pool is full of rain water washed off the hot cracked concrete paths. The water is deeper, with a tinge of Prussian to its depths. I spend a bit of time experimenting before I decide, yes, that I'll keep the teal and add the Prussian. My Prussian pencil has hardly been used. I smile.

'What's so funny?'

Mum is standing in my doorway, an imitation grin on her face. I open my mouth to explain but shake my head again. I don't think she'd get it. Instead, I hold up my sketchbook and show her the pool. Because I haven't added anything but the water to the page, I see her look puzzled. She shrugs.

'Thought you might like to go to this.' She comes over and hands me a pamphlet. 'We'll have dinner when Dad gets home.'

'Is Dad with Max?'

Mum looks at me strangely. I guess I don't need to ask because Dad's so often with Max at the pub or the club or wherever they go. It's what he does on Saturday afternoons and sometimes into the evenings as well. I've never met Max even though he's Dad's only friend that's not from his work. Ever since I'd been old enough to be told about the club and its flashing, dazzling poker machines, I've known about Max.

I take the pamphlet. 'What is it?' I say, waving it at Mum.

'Read it and you'll know. I can book you in on Monday.' The phone rings and she walks away, the draft from her leaving making the door pull shut.

The pamphlet is from Sunni Community Centre, a place in the city where they run different sorts of courses like *Indian cooking* or *How to buy things on eBay*. Mum has circled one in black pen: *Drawing class with Sam Keally*.

I leap off the bed and go out to Mum who's just hung the phone up, probably on a tele-marketer by the cranky look on her face. 'Can't you ring *now*? What if it gets booked out?'

'This only came out on Friday,' Mum says, taking the paper from me and looking for details. 'I'll do it Monday.'

'It's in the city.'

'I realize that.'

'You'll drive me there?'

'I wouldn't be showing you this if I wasn't prepared to drive you.'

I take the pamphlet back. 'Thanks, Mum.'

'You're welcome.'

I study the information and see that it's sponsored by *Keally Artworks*. 'Seems a bit sad that an artist has to make a living out of workshops and selling sketchbooks.'

Mum shrugs. 'At least it means he isn't working as a waiter.' She turns away into the kitchen.

I go back to my Prussian blue and make the pool a little bigger, a little deeper. My sketchbook balances on my knees and I can feel the embossed *Keally* across its cover. Sam Keally is a legend, famous for drawing small things big – the eyes of a praying mantis, bottlebrush flowers, bird beaks. He only offers two drawing classes a year, usually in Sydney where he lives. I've watched a doco on him. His drawings caught colour like no drawings I'd ever seen, even though I admit I haven't seen much. I just thought, from seeing him on the television, that he'd understand. I mean, understand *me*.

After that, the pool picture just poured out of me. I put Bull in the water, then again on the diving board, and then running around to join the queue. I blurred him so all you could see was the way he kept doing it, around and around and around. I made the others sit with their backs to him so they didn't notice what was going on. They were bright in the sunshine, their towels the colours of rainbows. All the normal kids sitting on their towels, clumped together. I draw a series of three pictures, the others leaving and the sun starting to go down until it was just Bull left, doing his thing without any thoughts in his head.

By the time I hear Dad come in, I'm drawn out. I lie on my bed on my back, staring at the milk-coffee ceiling. Bonnie drifts into my head, small and shy and wafer-thin, but I push her away. Why would Bonnie want anything to do with me when she can have Jordan? Nothing's ever going to change that.

5

BULL

'Pinch, punch, for the first of the month.' I get Dad on the arm, leaving quick red marks on his freckly skin. He laughs loudly, not even trying to slip and slap me back. He drains his coffee cup and sets it down with a clunk.

'What's on for Monday, Will? What's happening today with my bloody musical genius?' he says as he stands, pushing his chair in and trying to ruffle my hair. His fingers snag on my curls and I wince. He laughs again, knowing exactly how it feels to have hair so short and fuzzy. I inherited his hair, his Hereford cattle locks. *That's why you called me Bull and got me stuck with this stupid nickname.*

'Nothing,' I say, pulling away from his meaty hands and thinking of the millions of things that are going on today. Double PE. Science, Music. Lunch time orchestra rehearsal. History. And after school I've organised a two hour shift.

'Well, enjoy.' Dad sweeps up his lunchbox that he packed last night with tins of sardines and three bread rolls. He's on a sardine fix. Remember the baked bean fix he had a couple of summers ago? Nearly blew us all away at Christmas. You said that your house stank of tomato sauce for three days after we'd eaten Chrissy dinner and left. Let me tell you, sardines are nearly as bad as beans.

'Wait,' says Mum, putting her hand on Dad's stomach before he can get out the door. Mum's not really short but she is compared to Dad. He stops, though, as if she's speared him. 'We haven't talked about exactly when we're helping Janet.'

'Tonight's still okay,' Dad says. 'I'll be finished by five.'

'I'm working,' I say.

Mum eyeballs me. 'Since when?'

I shrug, casual as shit. 'I'm standing in for Kendo.'

Dad looks at me as well. They've got me pinned.

'When you finish,' says Mum slowly, 'go straight to Janet's.'

I eat some toast.

'See you there, William,' Dad says. He takes Mum's hand so that it leaves his stomach, gives her a slobbering kiss on the cheek (Mum smiles) and leaves.

I don't want to be alone in the kitchen with Mum so I stuff the rest of my toast in my mouth, fake horror at the time, and pack my plate into the dishwasher. By the time I've done that, collected some apples, two muesli bars and some raisin bread for lunch, El and Sofie have hit the kitchen, arguing like they do most mornings about who's been in the bathroom for too long. Mum turns her searchlight gaze to them and I'm free.

I go past the piano and can't resist sitting down and running my hand along its yellowing ivories. I practise a bit of Chopin, his chromatic étude, Opus 10 number 2. I play three bars over and over, trying to get faster as I go. I wish I could play better, that my fingers would work magic on the keys like his did. I like Chopin; I like the stuff he wrote. I think he was amazing, a *real* musical genius. This is *not* a cool thought so I don't tell anyone. I didn't tell _you_, that's for sure. I try the bars again as quickly as I can, muck them up, and leave it for now. An étude is a technically difficult piece and I don't really expect to ever get it.

In my room, I take the guitar from its stand and strum some chords. There's a new song on the radio, so you wouldn't know it, and I'm trying to work it out by ear. I make a mental note to Google it but I think I've got the basic rhythm. I flick the amp on, play it again with volume. It sounds okay. I sing a few lines under my breath to give it some guts, wishing that I had a voice like Morgan at school. Morgan's the singer in our lunchtime band and is way more talented than any of us. I've heard him sing solo. He is strong and loud and confident, the complete opposite of me. Morgan only sings with us because his sister is our drummer and he couldn't say no to her without being in serious brotherly trouble.

El's at the door, my serious sisterly trouble. 'Come on,' she says. 'You're late.' She disappears.

I walk them to school now. I have to take Sofie to her primary school first so I don't go to school the way we used to. It takes fifteen minutes to get to South Telford Primary, then five more to get to South Telford Secondary College. El and I go in the back gate and she heads off to her locker. That's a good thing because she doesn't see me go the long way around to class. I don't use my locker anymore. I got used to slinking in with my bag and taking it with me so that I could run off as soon as the bell went. The locker area is a no-go zone because it's one of those places that reeks with the fact that you're not there anymore.

There are four no-go zones like that. 1: the lockers. 2: your bedroom. 3: the tree in the park where you died. 4: the hidden hut in the bush that only you were allowed to visit. Thinking about those four places makes me feel sick so I try not to, but I have to because otherwise I'd forget to avoid them. Thinking about forgetting to avoid them makes me feel sick too. I think about accidentally finding myself at the no-go areas and my stomach lurches like I'm going to puke.

I feel a bit like throwing up now. When I get to class, Mr Gill says, 'Hi, William. You okay?'

I give him a nod. I'm just fine, Mr Gill. I swallow hard and make it through the morning.

I DON'T SEE Lewis until lunch. He isn't in any classes of mine except Maths and History. He comes in to orchestra with his trumpet dangling from his hands and gives me a lop-sided grin. I see at once that he's not focused. We're playing a new piece, getting it ready for the Term 2 ensemble concert. Lewis sits in front of me and barely raises the instrument to his mouth. When the bell goes for afternoon classes, he's the last to stand up. I leave my double bass on its side and go over to him.

'Hey, Lew. What's up?'

'Hey, Bull. Nothing much.' He looks at me with clear eyes and I see that he is alright but just in one of his Planet Lewis moods. He learned it in hospital years ago. I reckon it's a defence mechanism for him, a way of spending the long boring hours waiting at the diabetic clinic without going crazy. A sort of drift away from reality. I wonder why he's doing it today. 'Do you want to go to the Mall after school?' he says. 'I need some stuff.'

Don't get me wrong, Josh. We don't go to the Mall to hang out. There are only two shops we go to: Muso's

World and Telford Art Supplies. 'Can't, mate,' I say. 'Working.'

He nods, slow as a hippie.

'Tomorrow, maybe,' I say. Pay day's today. Money in the bank by tomorrow.

'Right,' he says, and walks out of the gym without looking back. I lug the school's double bass to the store-room, stand it up against its pegs, and wait for a minute. I didn't bother with the light and the store room is dark. Instruments line all the walls except for one where the drama costumes hang. I've used this store room many times as a safe haven, sitting at the bottom of the velvet dresses and capes and suit pants left over from past years' plays. I've never been discovered, even when someone flicks the light on. No one ever looks at the bottom of the costumes where my feet would be sticking out in their scuffed black school shoes. I've learned to slow my breathing to a shallow movement of air that won't stir any dust. The storeroom makes me invisible.

I'm tempted to sit here today but, really, school isn't my problem at the moment. It's when I finish the day that I'll wish that I was back here breathing in the musty, never-washed costumes with nothing but my own blood pumping through my body to keep me company.

AFTER SCHOOL I make my way to Speedy Sam's Burgers. I've had this job for exactly four months and five days. That means I've been off probation and onto the next level of wages for five days. Not exactly the millionaire pathway we used to talk about but with a crap job like this, any promotion acts as motivation to keep me turning up to the stupid shifts they give me. I walk in the back room, change into my dull green shirt (known as the booger shirt), and enter the Kingdom of the Kitchen.

'Here at last, princess?'

'Hello, Michelle.'

Fantastic. The Bitch Lady is manager today. She and I get on like a killer whale and a seal. I feel the cloud try to get me again but I push it away with an effort that makes me wince. Michelle snorts. Somehow, I've confirmed her worst beliefs about me.

If you had been around, we could have worked this job together.

'Piss off, Michelle,' you would have said with me standing right next to you.

Yeah, piss off.

I might be taller than her but I can't look her in the eye.

'Grill,' she throws at me.

I take an apron and head for the fatty end of the kitchen.

You know, I like this job. I like the boys out the back. We have good times, pickle fights and tomato sauce squirting competitions. If only the Michelles of the world would leave us alone.

The time goes quickly. I don't look at the clock but keep my head down turning out the meat patties. It's about half past six before Michelle notices that I'm still here and she grabs my arm. Her hand is podgy and soft and can barely grasp me. She lets go as if she notices her weakness.

'Get out of here, wanker,' she says. 'Don't think you're gonna get paid extra by working late.'

I duck away, take my time getting out of my oily apron and booger shirt, but have to leave eventually. Outside, the air is hot but at least it doesn't smell like fat. I shake work from me and consider what to do next. Too late. My phone rings (number 75). It's Dad.

'William,' he says without the usual niceties, 'where are you?'

'Just finishing work,' I say truthfully.

'Head to Janet's now,' he says. 'We'll see you in ten minutes.'

He hangs up before I get a chance to give him a useful reply like *no way*. Dad never asks anything of me, never suggests that I work harder at school or play soccer instead of the piano or even help Mum around the house (although he probably should do that). It seems he's got a bit shitty about this Aunt-Janet-moving thing and me trying to get out of it. Maybe he notices me more than I think.

It takes fifteen minutes to get to Janet's. I tell myself that my legs are tired from standing at the grill. Anyway, whatever it is, they don't seem to be working very well. I get there. Eventually.

Your house is just an ordinary one, pretty much the same as every house in the street. Sixty years ago I reckon it would have been quite modern. Today it's worn out. Dirty white weatherboards, green iron roof, slumping eaves. The front door opens to a corridor and rooms branch off either side. Lounge on the left, Aunt Janet's bedroom on the right. Kitchen on the left after that, Taylor's opposite. Bathroom on the left, your room next to Taylor's. Everyone's door usually open except yours.

Taylor moved out last year to go to uni. You always said he was the smart one of the family. I don't think he's that smart but he knows where he wants to go. Taylor is studying radiography and I can see him sitting in a dark room somewhere surrounded by pictures of people's bones and livers and brains. People can only study radiography in the city so he went, no fuss, and that's where he stayed. Even in the Christmas break. He works at Myer in the men's clothing department on the weekends. It's sort of weird thinking about him measuring inner legs but it's where he ended up. Better than burgers, I guess.

Taylor moving meant Aunt Janet was alone with the ghost of you in the house. I don't blame her for moving. I think she's stuck it out for too long and I wonder why. Just get out, go. Put one hundred kilometres between the house and a new start. I wish I could.

'Hey, Will,' Dad calls out cheerfully from the front door.

Maybe it's the sight of Dad in the doorway, looking familiar and solid and so much part of my life. Maybe I saw a shadow in one of the front windows – Janet peeking out from behind a dusty curtain. Maybe my head just finally registered where I was. Anyway, the cloud that threatened at work comes crashing over me. I freeze on the footpath, knees locked, jaw clenched, wondering whether I'm going to piss my pants like I did the day you died. Dad is speaking, his lips are moving. I can't hear.

The cloud rolls on a bit and my legs get back their movement. They turn me around. I start to run. My bag crashes around on my back and sweat seeps into my shirt but I'm running so fast it doesn't have a chance to drip.

Catch me, Bull!

I run all the way home, sprint up the driveway, bash through the laundry door because it's always open, and make it to my bedroom. I drop my bag, turn on the music as loud as it goes and pull the door shut, the curtains closed. Then I go under my doona, sweating more, eyes closed, breathing hard and fast and hotly. My brain is seizing with the heat but I concentrate on the bass line in the song – boom boom bom bom boom – until it overtakes what I'm thinking.

And what I'm thinking is that you've totally stuffed up my life, Josh, and I'm never going to get it back.

———

Mum, Dad, Sofie and Ella come home about eight o'clock. They walk in the front door and go to their various household places.

Mum's in the kitchen, clattering.

El turns on the telly to watch the latest terrible soap.

Sofie is brushing her teeth – nearly her bedtime.

Dad heads to the shower. I hear him turning on the radio to catch the sports results.

When I think everyone has settled, I open my door. Ella turns her head to look at me briefly when I sit on the couch. Mum comes and presses a plate of warmed up pasta in my hand. Sofie puts her cheek on top of my head to say goodnight. When Dad comes out of the shower, he sits next to me smelling of soap. He pats my leg once and we watch the horrible program in front of us. No one says anything to me about my escape home. They've been instructed not to by the family therapist we go to once in a while.

But Dad breaks the spell. After a while, he stands up to get a cup of tea and he wraps me in a one-armed neck hug. I inhale his clean Dad-smell of cheap aftershave and Johnson's baby powder. He says, 'Time will make it better, mate,' before he strolls to the kitchen like an overgrown grizzly bear. I feel my heartbeat slow, my body give a bit and I'm a little bit human again.

6

LEWIS

W rong, wrecked, rotten. The words appear in my head surrounded by flashing scarlet lights as I tear up my pictures of Dad from Sunday night. Something wasn't happening and these drawings are bad. I have a squinty-eyed last look but there's no hope for them. They won't sit on the page right. They're skewed. Dad looks like he's going to fall off his armchair onto the floor. He has a strange look on his face – maybe he feels a bit seasick? It's hard enough to draw Dad with the right look on his face so I can't leave him with this one.

Dad doesn't say much to anyone at any time. He's a man-of-few-words, says Mum, like not talking is a disease. I don't know him any different. If he started saying more than two sentences at a time, I'd die of fright. I don't know what Dad thinks of me drawing because he's never said. If he comes across something I've done – maybe in my open sketchbook – he looks and his head nods once but I don't really know what that means. Sometimes he'll say 'That's okay' and I figure he likes it. Still, I wouldn't want him to come across any drawings of him that don't look like I've tried my hardest to get him right.

It had always been a chance that these drawings would be wrong because I was doing them in daydreamer mode. Sometimes good drawing comes out of daydreamer mode. When nothing else matters but the whirling images in my head, the drawings are good.

Damn good.

Fantastically, extraordinarily, magnificently good.

Not yesterday. My head was fine, my body not. When daydreamer mode is because of how my body is, nothing works well.

It's what pisses me off the most about my diabetes.

'You're *travelling well*,' said the school nurse last time he saw me.

Yes. Carefully balanced meals, more carefully balanced medication. Regular blood glucose level testing. I know what to do, I've read the books. I've been a good boy, no late nights, no excessive stress, no strenuous unintended exercise. No sex, drugs or rock 'n' roll. And even so – what the hell? – my body has failed me. My toe hurts and drips green stuff. My BGLs do this dip and rise thing for no reason at all. It just isn't fair.

Blah.

I'd come home after school feeling wobbly and gone straight into drawing with a red pencil. Chrome red, midnight sun – the most toxic of all chromate pigments. When I draw, I sometimes think of how these colours came to be named. Of course, my pencil is not toxic but it's named after something deadly. I like that. Today I feel a bit deadly myself.

The boy with the school bag had left the page but there were others waiting to be drawn. A tall guy, hair over his face, skinny as a garden stake. I'm not sure who this new dude is but he was the only picture to come out. So I'm drawing away with my toxic red when I felt my own body waver and finally crumble. I had to go and fix me up. The sketchpad dropped to the floor and that's where I'd found it just then and decided to get rid of yesterday's Dad.

I finish ripping and drop the strips of paper into the bin and sit cross legged on the bed, listening. Mum is still at work, Dad's gone to the pub. The house isn't talking, keeping its creaks and squeaks for a windy day. I wonder what Sam Keally is drawing at the moment. I pick up my pencil and run it lightly over a new page, waiting for the tall, skinny guy to come back but all that's appearing at the moment is a sketch of my own desk. My Maths textbook is still open at the problem page I rang Bull about days ago, a leaking pen glues itself to the paper. For some reason, my blue zip-case full of diabetes stuff is on my chair – it usually sits in the top drawer of my bedside table. I scowl at it but draw it in. Even though it's small, it seems to take up the whole page. I sigh, stop and turn over a page to a clean start.

Finally, the tall boy appears. He's just standing on a corner, hands in pockets, his head tilted to one side. His face is blank, no smile, nothing. It dawns on me who it is. Me. Is this how I really see myself?

Mum comes home. The house breathes a sigh of relief and starts evening noises. She yells out to me, 'Lewis, everything okay?'

I think about lying. 'I'm fine,' I finally say knowing I've given it away in that small silence before I answered. The clatter of crockery slows for a moment but speeds up again. I hear Dad come through the back door. His deep voice is warm and happy. 'Hello,' he says to Mum. The pub and probably Max have done their trick. I don't hear Mum saying anything.

I slam the sketchpad on that boy inside, fit the chrome red back in its box and leave my room to join the sounds of dinner. It feels safer out there.

7

BULL

'Then she said…'
       'And I told him…'
'…last time.'
'Did you see…?'
'…not a chance.'

The science room is buzzing with bits of useless conversations by the time I get there. It runs together like white noise. I'm not late for any particular reason except, of course, that I was avoiding the lockers. Mr Henderson doesn't notice. He's handing out papers and puts one on the desk in front of me before I even sit down.

'What's this?' I ask Kendo.

He shrugs, ears plugged and fingers tapping to a beat that I can hear from half a room away (but didn't make it to my list).

Charlie is at my other side. 'It's a thing for mapping out your family,' he says. 'You know, like they do for racehorses and greyhounds.'

Yeah, well, Charlie would know all about that. Charlie is sixteen but he looks eighteen. It's hard to say why

7

because he's shorter than me and he still has braces. I think it's his face: it's square, like his Dad's, and he's got more beard hair than the rest of the class put together. Dressed in his brother's bank work clothes, Charlie gets away with buying beer and putting bets on at the TAB. He knows more than the average about racehorses and greyhounds.

'Don't they just use the same sperm for all the top race-horses? Even stuff from dead horses?' Kendo leans across me to get to Charlie and punches him in the arm.

Charlie rips out Kendo's earplugs but the music's off anyway. 'No, you idiot. And even if they did, it doesn't guarantee you've got a horse that actually wins stuff. You need a good trainer, jockey…' Charlie's in full flight. I tune out and study the paper.

It's a series of squares and circles. I see Mr Henderson pull up a diagram on the whiteboard and, over Charlie's blah blah about artificial insemination and the benefits of high protein racehorse food, I hear our teacher talk about filling in the shapes with the names of your relatives. 'Okay?' says Mr Henderson, completely ignoring or totally deaf to Charlie. 'It's called a genogram, a family tree. Have a go at filling in the names of your family that you know.'

'Jeez, that'll be quick,' mutters Kendo who has never known his dad except by his Mum's description of him as a First Rate Loser. As I look, he puts 'FRL' in the box for his father and 'Grand FRLs' in the boxes for his father's parents.

I turn back to my paper but keep half an eye on Kendo. He has his chewed pen end in his mouth as he thinks about his mother's side, and takes it out to print single words. Mum. Gran. Pops. Christine (sister of Mum). Celeste (sister of Christine and Mum). He *says* he doesn't give a shit about his father but I don't know if that's true.

There's a lot of blankness on that side of the page. A lot of unknown. It would make me feel strange.

Mr Henderson lets us go for another five minutes. 'Right, class, finish it at home with the help of your significant others.' Mr Henderson always says *significant others* when he means parents. He's the only teacher in school who calls Parent Teacher Interviews *Significant Others Interactions*. He's very PC and totally weird.

'You haven't done much,' Kendo says, looking at my paper. I'd put in Dad's three brothers, my four girl cousins, and Grandpa and Nan. Nothing on Mum's side. I didn't really want to think about Mum's side because it leads, of course, to you.

'I'll do it later. Can't remember everyone's names.'

Kendo shrugs.

Mr Henderson is talking again. I wish I'd tuned in a bit sooner because he's saying something about blue eyes and brown eyes and the possibility of being born with them. My eyes are changeable – green or blue or even this light gingery brown depending on the day. This fact distracts me and I miss the entire point of what he's talking about. I glance at Charlie but he's drawing a thoroughbred pedigree on his genogram, giving the circles and squares horse names like Blazed Lightning and King of Condor instead of his mum and dad. So I look at Kendo. He's listening, sort of. As well as Kendo *can* listen. I make a mental note to ask him later what's going on.

The class finishes in a rush of action as people jam out the door to get to lunch. It's been a long morning, with assembly taking up a lot of the first period followed by History. I used to think History was alright until we got Mrs McWilliams as a teacher. She must be one hundred and ten years old. Her idea of History is to pound you over the head with a textbook while making you repeat the death dates of past and forgotten kings. History this year is more like Maths. I crash out the door with the rest of the class because I need food in that empty, it's-been-too-long-since-I-last-ate, way.

Lewis is already sitting in the quadrangle, legs stretched out in front of him like two brown tree saplings. The Year 7 kids have to step over them as they pass but he doesn't shift. I grin at him and he gives half a smile back. His cap is pulled over his dark eyes but he knows what he's doing. He's taking up space. It's the way he copes with the length his body has grown. He's so tall now that I bet he gets giddy looking down at his feet. Thin, though. Thin like a burnt stick. Complete opposite of me.

'Hey, Lew,' I say with a mouthful of sandwich.

'Bull,' he says without looking up.

I sit next to him and concentrate on stuffing things in my mouth. God, I get so hungry these days that I sometimes wonder if I'm not full of tapeworms. 'I saw this photo once,' I say to Lewis. 'This girl had tapeworm. Someone held a plate of steak up in front of her. Tapeworms can smell meat. One crawled right up from her guts and came out her mouth. The picture was a man pulling it out – it must've been two metres long.'

'Jesus!'

That story always makes me feel a bit sick. I wish I hadn't mentioned it. I look sideways at Lewis. 'Eaten anything?'

'Yes.'

I nod.

Kendo rocks past, sees us, stops and drops onto the seat. 'Got anything to eat?'

I hold up my empty plastic bag. Lewis shakes his head.

'Got any money then?'

I've got ten dollars in my wallet but I'm not giving it to

Kendo. He never brings enough food to school and is always asking for money. I shake my head. Lewis shakes his again.

'Shit,' says Kendo and leans back, sighing.

Jules and Grace walk past and we watch them. Jules gives us a distracted look but she's too busy talking to stop. I watch Grace's hair bounce as she brushes it back over her shoulder as if it's annoying her. It's so curly and dark. It looks soft. I turn away but see out of the corner of my eye that she's stopped and turned to us. Jules walks a pace by herself and then grinds to a halt.

'Kendo,' Grace says. 'Tell Jules what it is that girls want.'

'Huh?' Kendo looks at Grace with a stupid puzzled face and she steps forward.

'I was explaining to Jules that people think boys don't know what girls want. But they do.' Grace reaches out for Kendo's arm and wraps her hand around his biceps. I see Kendo straighten a bit, flex that muscle under her grip so that her fingers have to dig in to stay there. 'Tell her.'

None of us are watching Kendo, we all have our eyes on Grace. Is it the way she's holding him with her stare or the way she's leaning forward, gripping him tightly as if she's not letting go until he answers? There's a pause as Kendo considers his answer. The wrong one and I think she might kill him. Death by bicep strangulation. The silence goes on. I try to think of ways to help him.

'Maybe…' I start to say and stop.

Now everyone's looking at me. Grace's hand slides off Kendo and he slumps back a bit, trying not to look too relieved. Grace has a snake drawn on her forearm. I can't look in her eyes so I keep them on the snake. 'What were you going to say, Bull?' she says almost so quietly I don't hear it. Almost so quietly it's a threat.

'Maybe they want the same as boys.'

Kendo snorts. He thinks I've given her the wrong answer and he's waiting for the blood. The snake coils around as Grace lets her arm hang down. Is she disappointed? I try again. Third time lucky. 'I mean, boys just want to be left alone. No stress. Same as girls. They want to be left alone to get on with things.'

This time, Kendo laughs loudly, Jules joining in a second behind because she's just noticed something's funny. But Grace doesn't laugh. Neither does Lewis. Grace stares a moment longer, gives me the smallest smile, then turns to go. Her skirt flicks out and I glimpse a hot, summer-brown thigh. Jules follows her. They disappear around the corner without looking back at us.

Kendo's laugh dies a natural death. We sit. I feel the heat that Grace always brings with her fade slowly away. The day rolls on.

'Working on the weekend?' Kendo asks me eventually.

'Saturday afternoon. You?'

'Sunday.'

It's good when Kendo and I are on the same shift but it hardly ever happens. I don't get why Speedy Sam's Burgers doesn't roster us on for the same time every week. They seem to like stuffing us around with an ever-changing-weekly-roster. It's probably the Bitch Lady. That's the sort of thing that would make her smile.

Kendo elbows Lewis in the ribs. 'You got a job yet?'

There's a beat, a milli-pause, the nanosecond space that it takes for a hummingbird wing to flap. Kendo doesn't notice. I do. Lewis says, 'No, mate. What do I need money for? I'm rich.'

Kendo splutters in mock horror but he doesn't ask any more. He's the sort of guy that only thinks about things when they're right in front of his face. It wouldn't even cross his mind to think that one of the things that Lewis wanted desperately was to get a job. Anywhere. Even at Speedy Sam's Burgers. But what he doesn't want to do is to tell a potential work boss that he has diabetes and that he might need help one day if things don't go the way they should. Telling a boss his darkest, blackest secret is the only way his mum will let him get a casual job. So it just isn't happening. Not yet. Maybe never.

I don't look at Lewis. He doesn't look at me. I think of Grace, I wonder about Grace, I wish I had my hands in Grace's hair. We stare into the school yard, watching the others as they go about their business of eating lunch and staying alive.

UNLESS I'VE GOT band practice, I have to walk Sofie home from school, too. Ella is almost always at netball or tennis or training for the Olympics so she can't do it. When I can't, Mum makes 'arrangements' with someone else. That is, arrangements with a mother who doesn't work all the time and has the freedom not only to get her own kid from school but also someone else's.

Today Sofie's late and I stand at the gate slapping my palm on the steel bar that keeps the primary school kids inside. I'm not allowed in the school grounds. There's a total ban on high school kids after a group of Year 7s got into a fight with some Year 6s last year. I mean, why would you waste your energy doing *that*? Anyway, it means that I have to stand outside and wait for Sofie while the other people – the Mums and Dads and Grandpas who've come to collect their darlings – can go in and get them.

Finally, Sofie comes down the path, her bag hanging off one shoulder like a forgotten jumper. Usually I reckon my little sister's kind of cute. Today she looks like a pain in the arse.

'Where have you been?' I snarl at her and she widens her eyes at me.

'Playing with Tom,' she says.

'Sofie, you need to come straight to the gate after the bell rings. You know I can't go in.'

'I wasn't very long. Me and Tom were looking for locusts.'

I start walking and she has to follow. 'Locusts?'

'Like the plague.'

Now I get what she means. Last year we had a locust plague and they hatched in the school sandpit. 'There aren't any locusts this year, Sofie.'

Sofie shrugs, her interest gone. She heaves her bag up and runs ahead of me. Her legs are skinny in her school shorts and look barely thick enough to hold her up. I wonder if I ever looked like that.

'Will,' she calls suddenly. 'Look!'

I turn my head to where she's pointing. It's Aunt Janet in her twenty-year-old Holden. She's pulled up at the kerb and waving at Sofie. Of course, my sister runs over. I stop where I am. I can see them talking, Sofie's head wobbling around as she nods and laughs. I feel strange, alone. I'm not sure why I can't cope with Janet any more. She has always been good to me, understanding my music, under-standing my strange-but-true hatred of all things sport. I stand on the footpath and feel myself spin away like I do sometimes, like my brain's leaving my body and leaving the shell standing there on the path. But I come shooting back when Janet gets out of the car and walks towards me.

You had her hair, like I got Dad's. Her hair is brown and straight and these days she wears it long, over her eyes. You always had yours in a clipper cut so it stood up from your head like warning spikes. She comes right up to me and I blink.

'William,' she says softly and goes to put one hand on my arm, changes her mind, drops her arm by her side. 'I'm all packed up. I've got some things for you, some books, a few clothes. I thought you might like them. I've given them to your Mum.' She pauses and smiles sickly. 'You know that I'm going on Friday.'

By Friday lunch time your house will be empty. By next week a completely strange family, one that won't know what happened and probably wouldn't care if they did, will invade it. Someone else in your lounge room, using your kitchen, sleeping in your bedroom. I nod at Janet. 'I know.' My voice is croaky as if it hasn't been used for a long time.

'I've got some things for you,' Janet says again but I can't answer. I know she means *your* things but I don't know whether I'll ever be able to look at them. She reaches out, takes a chance, and hugs me. In my ear, she says, 'I'm having a farewell dinner on Thursday. Fish and chips because all the saucepans are packed.' She gives one hollow laugh. 'Come along, Will. Please.'

She doesn't wait for an answer but lets me go, turns to stroke Sofie's head, and gets back into the Holden. We wait while she takes off to wherever she was going before she saw us then start heading home. Sofie hums a song and it's vaguely familiar, probably one from when we were really young. It gets into my head and by the time we reach the gate at home, I'm humming too. Sofie gives me a real smile – a little girl smile full of gums and teeth – and she's cute again, after all.

8

LEWIS

'Will here do?' Mum points to a chair at the doctor's. I nod. We both sit. Mum picks up a magazine but I just look around.

I know this room almost as well as my bedroom. It hasn't changed in the five years I've been coming here as a regular and reluctant customer. Dr James is predictable and sensible. Her surgery shows this. The walls are white-rendered plaster with mission brown window trims. Mission brown beams run across the ceiling. The toys in the corner are solid - primary red, blue and yellow - and can withstand a dishwasher. The latest magazine is dated 1999, almost antique. I've read it at least ten times.

Despite the blandness – because of the blandness – I reckon this waiting room is comfortable, reminding me a bit of a tree house that might have been a favourite play place years ago. The waiting room at the city hospital, for all its relaxing pastel colours and game station in the corner, is terrifying. There, I can't do anything but concentrate on breathing. In, out. And again. In, out. In my doctor's waiting room, I can find pictures I've drawn of Dr

James and the pointy-nosed receptionist called Donna in the margins of ancient *National Geographics* and *Vogues*.

Today I'm here because of my toe. Again. Before that, I hadn't seen Dr James since last November. I grew twenty centimetres and put on four kilograms over summer. That's holidays for you, all that swimming and sunshine and hanging around without school on my mind. Because I'd grown so much, they had to change my medication. I went to the city for that, to the child health hospital diabetic outpatient clinic, the CHHDOC. Chhhhhhhhhdok. Our little local hospital doesn't deal with people like me. The city hospital is a three hour drive and a three hour wait in the pale blue waiting room with all the others like me. Dr James looks after me in between visits to CHHDOC. 'Why can't you see me all the time?' I asked her once but she just shook her head at me. 'You need to see the experts, Lewis,' she said. I don't know about that. *She* is an expert on *me*. What else matters?

'Lewis. Miranda.'

Dr James is calling us in. I stand up, Mum beside me, and we walk behind the large broad back of Dr James to her room where mission brown paint is a feature as well. I sit in the chair next to Dr James's desk while Mum sits back against the wall. I can't remember when this happened, when Mum started to step away from the front line. It doesn't matter, she's still in the room, and Dr James does a great job of talking to us both.

'Lewis.' Dr James folds her hands on the desk and looks at me squarely. 'How's it going?'

This is shit, I want to tell her. I'm on twice as much stuff as I was and my blood sugar freaks out for no reason and I'm sick of this and I'll have to do it forever. I feel really strange lately and I've got no idea why. Oh, and my toe is oozing green stuff despite the horse-tablet sized antibiotics you put me on two weeks ago.

'Fine,' I say and don't look at Mum.

Dr James doesn't believe it for a moment but she nods and checks this, checks that, looks at my book, taps into her computer, asks about my diet, my exercise, my trips to the diabetic educator, the new medication. I answer in facts, truthfully, and let Mum say her piece. Dr James studies my toe with a sort of medical relish that seems a bit weird (ulcerated pus-filled toes are *not* exciting) and then puts my foot back on the bed. I wait for the verdict. She looks up with that look on her face that I know really well.

'No,' I say before she can say what she has to say. Her face swims a bit in front of me. 'Not this week. I'm going to Sam Keally's drawing class.' Mum got me in – she kept ringing Monday until she got through on the phone. Sam Keally is a legend. I can't miss this. I stare at Dr James, willing her to get it. I stare at her and wait for Mum to say something. She doesn't say a thing. I realize that neither Mum nor Dr James would think Sam Keally is anywhere near as important as a hospital admission for a disgusting pus toe that just won't heal.

'There's no choice,' Dr James says frankly because frank is her middle name. 'We've waited too long already. We don't want this to get worse.'

Can it get worse? Of course, everything can get worse. I know that, I've seen it in the hospital. The complications from this thing I have are many and disgusting. I'm probably on my way to ketoacidosis right now. I grind my teeth, feeling myself swing low and angry, but don't say anything. I understand. I just don't want to. I want it all to go away.

BACK AT HOME briefly before Mum takes me into school, I go to the dark sanctum of my room. Out of habit, I pick up my sketchbook and hold it open at the last drawing. The page is blurry. I'm not crying or anything, but I can't see straight. I make out me on the page. I pick up chrome yellow, the colour of taxi-cabs, warning signs on roads and Dr James. Safety yellow. I sketch in the doc leaning on the wall behind me. Next to her, suddenly, is Mum. They both have the same expressions on their faces – a sort of watching and waiting look. I should feel protected but instead I feel like I've lost something.

'Ready to go, Lewis?' Mum yells from the kitchen.

I think Mum's asked a straightforward question. Or is it a coded one? Sometimes when I talk to Mum I'm not sure what we're meant to be saying to each other. 'I'm just getting my school bag.' I hope that wasn't code for anything weird.

She clatters on. I can hear her putting breakfast things away. We must have had a normal conversation then. I leave my room and Mum gives me a smile. It's such a tired sort of smile that I almost stop in my tracks and sink to the floor in sympathy but she grabs the car keys. 'Let's get the rest of the day on the road,' she says briskly, The Judge again.

So we ride off into the sunset towards the rest of the day while the wheels turn around me and the hospital gets ready for a new arrival and Sam Keally's workshop has a sudden vacancy.

9

BULL

'Right. Look at me. Watch for my call. Ready? Strings? With us? Right. One two three.' Mr Sinclair slices his baton through the air.

Our new piece for orchestra is from that hit pirate movie. It's dark and complex but at least we know what it should sound like because we've all seen that film, even Lewis who doesn't have a lot of time for screens. Whenever we learn themes, I can never watch that movie again without hearing the soundtrack over everything else (I have three movie soundtracks on my list). The actors say whatever but I can't hear them without putting their words behind the tune. It's really annoying but it's sort of fascinating too. Without the music, their lines are often crap. Without music, everything is bland.

Lewis is over to my right. I can see the bell of his trumpet sticking through the crowd of stands and kids. He's been quiet today, hardly said a word in Maths. Not that he says much anyway. I know he prefers to draw rather than speak, that his pictures are his words. I can hear him playing, though. I can hear all parts of the orchestra, know when they should be in or out, but I hear Lewis more. If he's playing like he should then at least I know that he's here, with us, in the current world.

The hour goes quickly. We like this piece even though it's tricky and we're dodge at it. Mr Sinclair is working hard out the front. He has a way of whipping his head around and staring at people who aren't concentrating but he hasn't had to do much of that today. He works his arms and body with the music and we start to pick it up. Afterwards, I heave the bass into my arms and head to the store room.

I don't notice Lewis until we get to the door and he reaches in to turn on the light.

'Shit!'

He shrugs. I put the bass in its rack and we walk out together. There's five minutes before class so we get drinks from the vending machine. I pay, I've got the money. Lewis drinks all of his before I notice what he's bought. 'Hey,' I say.

He shrugs again. It must be okay.

He's studying his can as if it's the first time he's seen it. 'I'm going into hospital tomorrow.'

It's not okay then.

'Why?'

'My toe isn't healing.' He stares into his can. 'I need IV antibiotics.'

I picture him rigged to a beeping machine being pumped full of drugs. 'How long will you be in?'

'I don't know.'

It's hot in the quadrangle so we move back into the shade, into the corridor that runs to the science rooms. Other kids move past us talking and shoving or just making a beeline for somewhere else. Lewis watches them. I see the way his eyes follow their movement, their freedom. I can see that he's thinking about not being here tomorrow. Slowly, the can crushes in his grip. As we go to class he throws it into the bin so hard that the bang makes the kids in front of us jump.

The whole gang is in History. It's the only subject we all have together. Our combined hatred of History this year means that it's a riot. I'd feel sorry for Mrs McWilliams if I didn't think it was her own fault.

Charlie and Kendo are at the back and they're having Fists – taking it in turn to punch each other until someone flinches. Charlie's pain threshold is higher than Kendo's and, despite Kendo's polished and toned bod, I know who's going to win before Charlie throws the next one. Kendo blinks just before the fist lands and he's down, yelling in pain. Charlie raises his hands in victory. I feel my own arm ache in sympathy with Kendo's. Charlie beat me last week and I've still got the bruises to prove it.

'I don't know why you guys keep doing that,' says Grace as I sit down behind her.

'That's because you're a girl,' I say. 'You're not meant to understand.'

'You mean, I don't *want* to understand,' she says and turns to the front. I get a whiff of her shampoo as her hair moves. Sweetness. Somehow, I don't usually think of Grace as sweet. She's beautiful but not sweet. More spiky than that. *Treacherous.* The word flashes into my head and I think that the pirate music might have put it there.

Mrs Mac comes in but we don't stop our talking. She goes to say something but instead turns to the whiteboard and starts writing. The girls strain to see what she's doing – even though they hate her, they still try. It's only early in the year. I wonder how long it will take before even they stop listening. Mrs Mac writes for so long that eventually everyone does shut up. She finally turns around.

'This is a year-long assignment,' she says, waving at the board. 'This is different to every other assignment you've ever done. I'm not going to mark it.'

There's a sigh of relief and a bit of laughter. She's not going to mark it? We're not going to do it.

Mrs Mac is not put off. She takes a handful of notebooks from her desk and starts to hand them out. 'These are blank, except for the first page. Apart from that, they're for you to fill in as the history of this year. A journal, diary, notebook – whatever you want to call it. These are your own and they don't have to be shown to anyone else.'

'This is crap,' someone says.

'Why are we doing this?' Someone else.

Mrs Mac sighs, the worn out breath of a teacher trying too hard. 'This is history – your history. What you write will be happening in the world around you now. It's a record of your time. You might want to put in articles from the newspaper, headlines from the news or lines out of books you're reading.'

'*A small mind is easily filled with faith.*' Kendo. A war gaming codex quote. They're the only things he reads.

Mrs Mac chooses not to hear. 'Or you might just put in your own thoughts of the world. Comments on the day. What you've done or what other people are doing.'

'Boring,' someone else says.

'Maybe,' says Mrs Mac. 'But maybe not. If you keep this book and read it back in five years' time, you might be surprised at what it says. There might be things in there that you would've forgotten. This assignment is one for the future. It's a time capsule. I challenge you to give it a go.'

More sighs, some groans, but also silence. I think that some of us like this. Mrs Mac hands me a blue notebook. I open it and see that there's a newspaper article stuck to the first page. The date is highlighted. Today. Mrs Mac has given us a head start. I close the book and look over at Lewis. He has a green one. He's holding it as if he's reading the front cover but all it says is 96 pages 8mm.

'What if we're already doing it?'

Mrs Mac is just about to go to the front of the room again. She turns to Lewis, eyeballs him thoughtfully, turns away. Lewis is still staring at the green cover. No one else seems to have heard him. 'If you're already keeping a journal like this one then you know what it's all about. You can carry on.' She reaches her desk, slams the three last notebooks on it, and says, 'William the Conqueror. What date did he die?' It seems that the bright moment of the class just went.

I forget about my notebook almost immediately. I think about Lewis's words for a moment longer – what was he talking about? - before they too fall from my mind.

I WAKE at two o'clock in the morning. I've been dreaming of the day I found you. Not the nightmare and not the details, just the feel. I remember it was a bright blue day, shimmering with heat. It was the day you turned seventeen, November 28th, fifteen months ago. It was so hot that sweat covered us even at breakfast. I had bought you a voucher from *Sports World* and it was ready in its red envelope on my desk. Everything was red about that day. That's what I dream about. The heat, the redness. The sight of you lying too still. Why, after all this time, aren't I over it?

Waking like this happens a lot. Even now, with or without dreams or screaming nightmares. I used to have a go at the things that the people who were trying to help told me to do - get up and have a drink, read for a bit, listen to the radio. Now I just lie in bed, doona up to my chin, eyes open and staring at the ceiling until my eyeballs dry out and I just have to close my lids. Sometimes it works. It doesn't tonight and I lie there until the light comes under the curtains and makes shadows in my room. I used to trust that the sun would make things better but now I know it doesn't. The sun makes shadows. That's not a good thing. I like the dark, complete blackness where nothing extra can get in.

One day until Thursday and I have to go to Janet's. It will be the last time I have to do it. There will never be another reason to go into that house where you once were. Will that be the only way I can do it, to think that I'll never have to do it again?

Mum gave me the things that Janet had for me. Your Rip Curl jacket. Your last edition of *The Guinness Book of Records*. A pile of music CDs, heavy metal, none of which had made my list. I put the taped-up box with everything inside in the garage behind a bin full of chook shit garden fertilizer. No one will find it there because no one does any gardening around here except when I get out there with the mower and chop the grass down to the ground. And that's only when Mum tells me (for the third time) to go and 'mow the lawns.' She gets so mad at me when I tell her we don't have lawns, we have weeds, but it's the truth. Mow the weeds, she should say.

I get ready for school feeling tired and irritable. Sofie knocks my bowl of cereal and milk spills on the floor.

'William, be more careful!' Mum yells at me.

'Me? It was her.' I point to Sofie.

'I didn't mean to,' Sofie says, her face darkening.

She refuses to talk to me on the way to school.

'You're a bully,' El tells me.

'Get stuffed,' I say to her. She stops talking to me as well.

It's not a great start to the day.

Lewis isn't here. The others automatically leave a space for him next to me in Maths so I end up sitting alone.

I get eight out of twenty-three for my homework sheet. I can't see where I went wrong and spend too long wondering about it and don't understand the rest of the lesson.

In English, my hearing seems to go. Music grows in my head, the rolling up and down waves of that chromatic opus, and threatens to drown out the rest of the world. I'm so tired my eyes feel thick. The lesson passes but I forget to go when the bell rings. That music is beating in time with the way blood whooshes around my body.

I only see Bonnie because she and I are the last ones left in the room.

'What?' I say to her after she mouths something at me.

'Are you okay?' she says. 'You're just…sitting there.'

'Is there a crime against that?' I say, standing up roughly and pulling my stuff off the desk. I can feel her watching me.

'Bull,' she says.

I pause but don't look up.

'Will,' she says, more softly.

'I don't have anything to say to you, Bonnie,' I say, matching her gentle voice. I walk around her, keeping clear. I'm almost away from her when she says, 'It wasn't my fault.'

I spin around, fury like vomit in my mouth. 'I *know* it wasn't your fault.' I bite down hard to stop me yelling.

It's Bonnie's turn to get mad. Her face glows red. 'So why won't you talk to me, Will? Why do you treat me like I don't even *exist*?'

'You've really got no idea?' I hiss.

'Absolutely no idea. None! I don't get it.'

'Well, let me tell you why.' My vision's gone weird - sharp and sparky - but I can still see her standing there, one hand on her hip. 'You don't have to act like he was never here *at all*.'

'I still don't understand.' Her voice is louder than mine but beginning to crack. I feel like I've scored a hollow victory.

'He was your boyfriend, Bonnie. And now you're with Jordan.' I swallow hard. 'How could you *do* that?'

'How could I do it?' She's shouting, hands clenched now and hammering at her side. 'How could *I* do it? How could *he* do it, Will. How could *Josh* do that to us? How could he have been so stupid as to die like that?'

'He was sick!' I yell. 'He didn't know what he was doing. He didn't mean to fall.'

She steps closer to me and all I can see are the rivers of tears on her cheeks. 'Well, he did, didn't he? He went and *died* on us. Why wouldn't he take his medication properly, why didn't he try? Why wouldn't he *listen*? All that shit I put up with because I loved him and he went and died on me!'

She's trembling and heaving and I don't want to look at her, I don't want to think about how she kept with you through your craziness when other people – not me, never me – couldn't. She sat with you the whole night at one of Taylor's parties while you talked about the importance of stopping greenhouse gases. *All night*. Watched you draw diagrams that made no sense, got you new paper and pens when you ran out. My head spins with the memory of it.

We stand for long seconds. She sobs. My breath heaves. They're the sounds of our pain. Finally, Bonnie shakes her head. 'And if I don't keep going, Will, then it's like I'm dead as well. Don't you see? You, of all the people in the world, should see that.'

My words are gone. I close my eyes so I don't have to see her anymore. Finally I hear her walk away, her breathing jagged and loud.

When I open them, I'm alone and my eyes are dry. I feel like throwing up but I don't. I realize that I don't do much these days, that sometimes I can't do anything at all. I take one breath in, let one breath out, until I'm as good as I get. Then I go out into the bright loud world of school and try and forget that I was ever alone in a room with Bonnie Valentine.

OUTSIDE, Kendo and Charlie are doing Fists again and I stay away. I wonder why it is that people do one thing over and over and over again and never realize that the same things will happen if they do. I see from a distance that Charlie wins. See?

I spend the rest of the day avoiding people. I even spend a bit of time in the storeroom – just one period – sitting in the dark and breathing in the costumes. No one notices me go in and no one notices me go out. It seems to help because I cope with the rest of the school day, make it to Sofie's school and take her home with the morning's trouble forgotten. Every now and then she grabs hold of my hand. Her skin is soft and I catch hold of her fingers until she pulls away to jump over a stone or walk along a low fence or stops to watch a bug on a fence.

Mum has left us a list of things to do for her so while I pick in the washing, Ella peels potatoes and carrots for tea. When my jobs are done, I shut myself in my room and pick up the guitar. In the hot afternoon light, its deep red surface shows all my fingerprints so I tilt it away, turn the amp down so that I can just hear it, and play a low soft noise until it falls into a tune. Minutes, hours, can pass this way and they do. It's no surprise when Mum pokes her head around the door. 'Tea time.' She gives me a smile – a good day at work for her then – and I mirror-smile back.

This blackened day is almost over. Only Thursday to go.

It takes four hours to drive to the city. There's an accident on the freeway in front of us and the detour takes us through hills, past farms and along roads that usually only see utes or tractors. I draw a little of it but the road is bumpy. We join back up at the outskirts of a town that has an abattoir. I just get a glimpse of the confused looks on cows huddled in a holding yard before Mum accelerates angrily into the freeway traffic. She hasn't had her coffee yet. It shows. It is a long four hours but we get there in the end.

We park in the gigantic multistorey carpark next to other ordinary cars. Families fill the hospital entrance. Little kids play on plastic slides in the foyer, babies cry in their mother's arms and Mums and Dads stand in groups - some happy, some sad. I study the faces of the sad ones as I walk by. I'm good at this – it comes with years of practice. I can tell which ones have just had bad news and which ones have been sad for a long time. The chronically sad ones have a heaviness that droops their shoulders as if the world is pressing in on them. I glance at Mum walking just in front of me. It's hard to tell from this angle but if I had to guess, I'd say that she was drooping inside as well.

All because of me, I know. All because of me.

Dad doesn't come to the hospital any more. The smells, the closeness of it, frightens him and he can't hide it even from me, his only kid. The Judge used to mutter about it, 'goddamnuselessman' but she can't be bothered anymore. She can take the weight of both parents' worry and a huge chunk of mine as well.

At this moment, Mum swings around. 'Come on, Lewis,' she says briskly but I am coming along. I know what she's doing, it's a sly move to check me out, to see if I'm still striding forward and haven't fallen soft under the spell of the hospital walls. I'm here, I'm here. I catch up to her so that we can walk together through the bright zinc white corridors. We go past the waiting room of CHHDOC and into the adolescent ward.

Unbelievably, I've got the same bed that I was in last time, even though that was two years ago when I had gastro and Dr James needed help to get me right. I'm trying not to think about how familiar the ward is because next to that thought is the panic I feel about being in here at all.

I put my clothes away, shove my backpack into the locker next to the bed and go to stare out the window. From here, I can see the high brick walls of the zoo. It looks like a prison and it is, in a *conservation* sort of way. Conserve the animals, keep them safe. I wonder whether they've ever been asked, would they prefer to be dead?

'Lewis, I'll be back in fifteen minutes.' Finally, Mum can get her coffee. I nod. 'I'll be right here, Mum.' That was obvious. Where else would I go?

She nods and leaves. I put one hand on the window to try to feel the day's heat but the double-glazing has kept the glass cool. Panic rises in my chest but I fight it down. It's only first- day nerves. I need to get used to being here. The colours just aren't mine, I'd never choose them.

The nurse looking after me waltzes in with a friendly smile and a genuine - maybe - interest in how I've been. 'How are you feeling, Lewis?'

I don't know this one but her badge says 'Tori.' 'I'm pretty good, Tori,' I say. 'Probably don't need to be here.'

She smiles. 'Well, you're here now. All going well, you won't be in for long.'

I look away. How long is too long? An hour?

When Tori leaves, The Judge returns. She tries not to but can't help herself and opens the cupboard anyway to fuss with the clothes that I just put in there. I watch her from where I'm standing at the window. All I can see is half her body and vigorous jerks as she pats my flat clothes flatter and puts one shirt on a hanger. When she can't do anymore, she shuts the door with a click.

'You don't have to stay, Mum,' I say.

'I know,' she says. 'I'll go and book into my room shortly.' She's staying at the Family Unit attached to the hospital. 'I'll leave you alone soon.'

But I like her there, even if she irritates me. In fact, this is when I like her the most. Brisk. Business like. Sorting out the shit from the manure, being The Judge. When the doctor comes, she gives him the third degree. 'What antibiotic will you use? How will it affect his insulin? Will Dr Nightingale check him today?'

I know the things she asks are important. Every now and then she stares at me as if she wants me to say something. All I do say is, 'I've brought my own stuff with me.' The doctor −Ravi, an intern − nods seriously as if that was the most important thing that I could have done. I can't say anything more because hospital dries my words up almost completely. I blame the glare of that zinc.

When he leaves, and Mum goes out to get her room key, I sit on the edge of my bed and stare at my toe. It amazes me how the simplest thing can lead me here. One stupid toe - not even my big toe but the one next to that. One stupid football game with one stupid slide in the gravel. Maybe even just one stupid germ in the gravel waiting to get into my system. When Tori comes in to set the drip up, she accidentally bumps the toe and I feel a stab of pain shoot through my whole leg. *There*, my toe seems to be saying. *Don't even think that I'm not important. I can be big trouble.*

Mum comes back, checks the IV line like a pro, reads a magazine while sitting in the visitor's chair until dinner arrives on its standard plastic tray. She watches as I eat everything they've given me – even the disgusting sugarless chocolate mousse – and then puts her hand on her own stomach.

'You go, Mum,' I say, pushing the bed table away.

She checks my empty dishes, the IV and me. 'Are you sure you'll be okay?'

I understand this code. It means, I'm leaving you alone in hospital now and I won't be back until the morning but would return in a flash if you wanted me. I give her an uncoded response. 'I feel like I know this place pretty well by now.' I don't hint at how much I hate it.

Mum nods. 'You'll be okay then.' She folds her magazine and stuffs it in her bag, leans over to put one hand on my arm and smooths the blanket with her other hand. She gives it a firm pat. 'See you in the morning.'

She goes. I sit staring out the window at the dusky sky and the prison walls of the zoo. When I finish with the window, I watch the ward. The other bed in my room is empty or should I say waiting emptily for its next victim. Nurses stride up and down the corridor propelled by important busy-ness that oozes out of their every pore. Tori has gone and Kim has taken her place, checking my drip, smiling at me, rushing off to his next job.

Finally, the long day finishes and I slide in under the cold, stiff white sheet. There's nothing I want to watch on the telly. Although I'm rigged up to a portable IV pole, the patient lounge has a sobbing boy in one corner and I don't need that. I've got my sketchbook on my lap but I don't open it until I can hear that someone is with the boy and the sobs slow.

There's a nice blank page in front of me and I draw in grey lead with part of my mind on the picture of the sad boy in the patient lounge, thinking that he'll come out on the page. He does, tears pouring down his face in a shadowy wash.

When I finish, I look hard at what I've done and decide that the boy is tired. There's something about the way he can't stand up properly but needs the wall, and how his left arm hangs down with his right hand around its elbow. He's tired of being in hospital, tired of being sick. Tired like me.

I fall asleep suddenly but not so deeply that I don't notice that Kim comes in and takes the sketchbook off the bed. He puts it on my bed locker with the pencil on top and I roll over so that when I wake up properly it'll be the first thing I see.

11

BULL

'Mapoutyourwholefamily,' Kendo talks to me about our science homework so fast I think he might be taking drugs. I stare blankly at the genogram in front of me with only Dad's side sketched in. 'Puthairandeye-colourin. Seewhatyouinheritedfromyourolds. Earsize,mid-digitalhair,longsecondtoes.' I can't do much more than I did the other day. I suddenly can't remember the colour of Mum's eyes. The thought worries me so much that I let time speed past.

Everything goes so quickly when you don't want it to. Thursday passes like a blur. Lewis is still away, still out of touch hundreds of kilometres from here. It's after school and I don't know how that happened. Even band practice flies past. Did I do anything? Was there any bass to the music at all?

I collect my bag, my guitar, my homework and time finally begins to slow down. There's nothing left to do but go home and then on to Janet's.

I imagine us grouped around her kitchen table silently

eating fish and chips. There won't be much to say. The house will be quiet around us. At least I'll have time to check out eye and hair colour and ear size and mid-digital hair and all those other things that are meant to be the special inherited presents from your family. And all along your room will be just down the hall, wanting me to glance in, calling me into its darkness.

Dad is waiting for me at home. I see at once that he's not having any of that panic attack nonsense. He pulls my bag from me and carefully puts the bass against the hall cabinet before he surrounds me with an arm and steers me to the car. I can't even change out of my sticky school shirt. Mum and the girls have already gone ahead, walking the few kilometres to Aunt Janet's. 'We're on takeaway duty,' Dad says, turning the car towards the centre of town. 'Fish and chips, right?'

The fish and chip shop we normally go to has closed down. No one in our family has noticed – that shows you how often we have takeaway. We get a roast chicken and packet salad from the supermarket, so from the start the night is different to what I had imagined. Dad collects bags of fun-sized chocolate on the way so that makes up for the lack of fun-sized hot chips.

When we get to Janet's, Mum, Sofie, Ella and my aunt are sitting on boxes on the veranda. The radio is playing softly in the background with number 62. I realize that there is no kitchen table. It's gone with all the big stuff. The house is being drained of your family, furniture and all. I think about how you were in the days before you got sick. Then I think about how it was when you were sick. The time you broke the window with your wild dancing that had gone on all night. The time you didn't get out of your bed for six days in a row. I remember too how sometimes you couldn't stand this place and so you disappeared into the bush, spending all day in that rotting wooden hut you found across the creek. No one else knew about it or if they did, you threatened them into forgetting. I kept that secret, like I'd kept your illness secret at first. It was another thing that I hid for you when I thought that you needed protection from everyone.

Big mistake. You needed protection from yourself. I didn't help you at all.

Janet is staring at me strangely as I walk up the path to the veranda. I almost panic and run but Dad is at my back. I stare at her blankly. 'Is your bed still here?' I say as the first thing that comes out of my mouth. I blush. She shrugs and answers like it's a normal question to be asked from your weird nephew. 'I left some cushions to sleep on for tonight.'

'You could come home with us,' says Mum as she takes the food from Dad and puts it on a tablecloth spread over three boxes.

'No,' says Janet. 'One more night.'

They look at each other, the sisters. I see that they have the same coloured eyes – blue, but that sort of blue that changes with the colours around them. Blue or green or hazel – like mine. I look at Dad. He's tearing apart the chicken, feeding greasy skin into his mouth. Dad has brown eyes, like Sofie and El. Mum reaches for Janet. Janet wipes at her face but when her hand comes down again her cheek is dry. Maybe she's okay? Mum makes herself busy by opening salad packets.

'Do you remember when Taylor wouldn't eat chicken?' says Dad, forking his salad in.

'We used to tell him it was beef.' Janet smiles.

'Why wouldn't he eat chicken but still eat beef?' says Ella. 'Beef is meat.'

'He saw the chicks at the Show. You know, the ones

they have in the incubator at the animal nursery. When he realized that we ate them once they were grown up, he refused to eat chicken.'

Dad shares a few more tales about Taylor. I eat as I listen, feeling the tension build in my shoulders and neck and head. They can't keep talking about Taylor without mentioning you. And then Dad says it.

'Josh could eat chicken. He didn't care. Remember he ate a whole dish of chicken legs that was meant to feed all of us?'

Catch me, Bull!

I close my eyes, my head pounds. The day slows right down almost to a standstill. I see Janet's fork on the way to her mouth. It wavers for a time-slowed moment but makes it there. She nods. 'Fourteen drumsticks,' she says. This time the tears do slide down her face.

Mum dabs at Janet's face with a paper serviette. Dad gives a wry, sad, crooked smile. Ella gulps. Sofie doesn't notice. And then it's all over. We finish our meal, everyone eating everything in front of them. The conversation starts again, drifts on, rolls over me. I peel wrappers off chocolates and pass them around. Janet takes hers, looks straight into my colour-matching eyes, and traces her thumb gently across the back of my hand. I don't pull back even though I want to.

'I'd offer everyone a cup of tea,' she says, sitting up and taking her hand away, 'if I had any cups left.'

'We'll cope without one,' says Dad. He stretches his arms over his head and looks out into the setting sun. 'What time are you going tomorrow?'

'I'll be out by eleven o'clock.' Janet leans back against the wall of the house. 'I'll be in the new place by this time tomorrow.'

'And I'll be up there to help you settle in next weekend,' says Mum.

'I'll look forward to that.'

We go quiet. I imagine Aunt Janet alone in a new house and wonder how she'll feel. Sad, because it's painful to go. Happy, because it's a new start. Confused, hurt, angry, about how she got there.

'Would you like one last look around?' Janet turns to Mum. 'There's still a box or two for you to take. Some of Mum's old things that I thought you might like.'

'And I promised to take some of your pots.'

'They're on the back porch.' Janet gets up. 'There's a few more than I thought.' She trails down the steps, Mum following, and they go around the corner of the house. Dad stands to go after them. 'Come on, Will. Looks like we'll be carrying pot plants to the car.' He lumbers away.

I stay with El and Sofie for a moment. Ella looks at me. 'This doesn't feel right,' she says.

I nod.

She sighs.

'Why?' says Sofie. We just look at her. Sometimes I wish I was seven again.

I go after Dad. He's already got four terracotta pots in his big strong hands. I dig in his pocket for the car keys and open the hatch for him. The pots tip over in the back, spilling dry musky dirt into the car. Dad grunts, sweeps the dirt back into the pots, and goes back to get more. Four trips and he's done. I arrange the plants so that they're jammed up against each other and can't fall, and push Dad's work jacket and an old towel up against them. I can hear Mum and Janet talking as they walk through the house and out the front door. Sofie and Ella give Janet a hug.

'A last look around?' asks Janet again, not looking at me.

I am a frozen iceberg and do not move.

'I'll say goodbye then.' She walks towards the car.

I defrost enough to go to her. She wraps her arms around me and squeezes. I'm not sure whether the time warp thing is happening again – was it too fast or too long? – but she lets go eventually.

'It's farewell, not goodbye,' says Mum. 'I'll see you next weekend.'

'Yes. See you then.'

Janet is looking at me as I get into the car. All I can see is the great black hole of the front door open behind her. Blackness. A house empty of you. A house silent without you. A house that used to be filled with your raging out-of-tune music, your great fits of chicken eating, your plunging, scary lows that left you sprawled on the floor flattened.

Ella's spot on. It's not right.

I EXPECT Lewis back at school Friday but he isn't. I make a note to text him at lunchtime and then remember I'm out of phone credit. I doodle in my Maths textbook and accidently cover some algebra exercises. I spend the next fifteen minutes trying to work out what I should be doing which means I'm fifteen minutes out of whack with the rest of the class. This shouldn't happen because I'm the one Lewis depends on when he's away. I have to fill him in on what he's missed so he can catch up. Especially with Maths. Maths is not Lew's strong point. It's not mine either but I'm better than him.

Lewis wasn't my friend until last year. Until after you died. He started at this school at the beginning of the year and was in four of my classes. I knew of him because I'd met him at an orchestra workshop but we weren't friends, hadn't even said anything to each other. We became mates when I was at my darkest. I'm not sure why but one day he sat beside me at lunch.

'Lewis Pascoe,' he said, giving his chest a mild thump.

I looked at him but took a while to focus. Back then, I found it hard to make things out clearly. A layer of greyness covered everything. I suppose I was silent because he said, 'William Healesville.'

'Healey,' I said automatically. 'Bull Healey.'

'Right,' he said, like that was a good choice of name. Like I had something to do with it. 'Related to Trigger Healey?'

The local football hero. 'No.'

'Right.'

I wished he would go away. I'd said more in that few minutes that I'd said all day. I felt exhausted.

'Skinny Healey?'

He was talking again. 'What?'

'Are you related to Skinny Healey?'

I knew of Skinny Healey. He played jazz. Trumpet. I shook my head.

'Too bad.' He looked almost cross about it.

'You play trumpet.' I said it without thinking. Trumpet was what he'd played at the orchestra workshop. 'You played Healey's *Mister Sometimes*.' Lewis had done a solo. No one else could play "Mister Sometimes," it was too hard.

'I tell them I'm a sometimes/but that's not true/I'm never a sometimes/and I'm not always blue.' He stopped singing and shrugged then leaned back against the wall. He wasn't so tall a year ago and his legs didn't stretch out far in front of

him. I noticed that he had a band on his arm, a sort of bracelet.

'What's that?' I nodded at it.

He looked down at his wrist and slid the band up his sleeve so that it was out of sight. 'Just my ball and chain.' He looked away at the kids playing four-square on the gravelly asphalt. 'I'm a prisoner, life sentence.'

I could have asked him more but I'd run out of words. When the bell went, we stood up together and went to English.

Since then, since I didn't have you, Lewis has been my closest friend. Not sure why, not sure how.

I phone his house from the one remaining public phone on the corner of the intersection nearest the school-crossing with the emergency phone card that Mum makes me carry. I have to sneak out because we need a pass to go outside the school gates at lunch. In my white polo shirt and navy blue shorts that shout *School Boy!* I stand out like bird shit on a black sheet but I take the risk. The phone rings and rings. No one answers. I hang up before the answering machine clicks in. I try his mobile. It goes straight to message bank. I hang up, defeated.

It's while I'm standing there that I think of your house. Janet said she was going at eleven o'clock. I look at my watch. 1:15pm. The house is empty now. Possibly the dust has already settled on the floor. All traces of you will be gone.

That's when I feel the pull. I can go to your house now before the strange family move in and I could check – one more time – that you're really gone and not just tricking us. The pull is strong and stupid. Crazy, even. I know you're not in your house. I might be mixed up about it all but I'm not mad. I'm not.

Before I can think it through, before I can come up

with some excuse or logic or block, I turn away from school and start on my way to Janet's. I don't look back to see if anyone's seen me.

I think: if Lewis was here I wouldn't be doing this.

But he isn't here and I feel lost. I go and see whether I can be found.

12

LEWIS

What does it feel like to go from sick to well? The hospital changes colour and becomes less stark white. Kim changes to Cindy and back to Tori and I begin to tell them apart. The food tastes worse, I'm not sure why. Mum smiles when she comes to see me and leaves early to have coffee with a city friend. The zoo walls don't seem as high and if I put my ear against the window I imagine I can hear screeches of creatures waiting for their dinner.

I've only brought an ordinary 2HB and so I have to make do with that. I try writing the colours instead.

Hospital Hues

Ocean blue with white caps
Sudden black with furry edges
Yellow again, egg yolk and sunny
Red pricks, white flesh
Grey as the outside sky
Rose warm inside the sheets
Until finally

Hair black
School boy white
Green earth, stable to light and air
Level again
For now

IT DOESN'T MAKE a lot of sense so I shade the whole page
to make the words less obvious. Words don't really capture
the pictures in my head. Words look like blocks. Ugly. I find
it hard to see words and imagine them as anything other
than sort of rectangular objects. When I finish shading, I
do a quick sketch of school, rows of kids at tables. Bonnie
sits next to Jordan and Bull is on the left of Kendo. I know
that's all wrong – Jordan doesn't even go to our school and
Bonnie shouldn't be with him anyway.

I think of Bonnie and the way her brown eyes are
sometimes dull when she thinks no one is looking at her. I
see them, they dim like she's turned the light down in
them. I watch her until she lights up again and wonder if
she hates having to be so falsely bright. I wonder, too, what
would let the light stay on naturally. Could it ever be me?

I turn the page quickly and start again.

It's Bonnie. I can't seem to help it.

I put my book away and wait for Mum to come and
get me.

13

BULL

'Hotter than a Jalapeno chilli in a blender full of Tabasco.' One of Dad's sayings and it fits totally.

It's one of the hottest days we've had all summer. This doesn't hit me until I'm far enough away from school to feel safe from being caught. I notice the sweat sticking my shirt to my back, the sun on my hair trying to burn my scalp, the squelch in my shoes as my feet melt. I think of the pool, its dark deep coolness. I sweat even more. Maybe if the pool was closer I would have detoured, dived in with my clothes on and felt the relief that comes from plummeting downwards into cold, blue water.

I keep walking without slowing. The pool is nowhere near here. I realize that I have to get back in time to pick up Sofie. If I come back straight away, I'll have heaps of time to pick up my bag and make it to the primary school. It should only take another five minutes to get to Janet's house. Janet's *ex*-house. Your ex-house. Well, it's been that for a while now. It hurts to think that way and I walk faster to keep ahead of the pain.

All these thoughts, and the fact that it is so hot Scouts

could fry bacon and eggs on the footpath, make me forget to keep track of where I am. And where am I? I'm suddenly right out the front of your ex-place.

I walk backwards until I'm under the tree on the nature strip. It's some sort of paperbark – old and shedding like a dog – but it shades me while I stare. There's no sign of Janet. The boxes on the porch are gone, her twenty-year-old Holden has left its oil stains on the driveway, the front door is firmly closed. The blinds are down. I think: what am I thinking? Of course the house is empty. It will also be locked. Did I think the door would be open and I'd just walk in?

But of course that's what I'd thought. And that's what I'm doing. I'm going to walk right in.

I ring the doorbell and wait and ring again and wait. Definitely no one there. I try the flyscreen door. Open. The wooden door. Locked. I push at it. Nothing. I move to the window and try the sash. Locked. I don't look over my shoulder in case someone is watching but I'm pretty sure that no one would be out in this heat. People will be inside with the blinds down and the air-conditioner on, trying to block out the summer.

I go around the back, swinging under the veranda's railing like we always do, and try the side window (locked), the bathroom window (locked) and finally the back door. I rattle it extra hard but it doesn't seem to make any difference. It's all locked, locked, locked and I'm still outside.

I look around for a brick.

What? Am I going crazy? I can't smash a brick into my Aunt's ex-house even if it *is* an ex-house. I thump my fist on the wall and dust flies out of the weatherboards and I remember our key.

The outside light is above the back door. I find some firewood stacked nearby and use an unsteady tower of it to help me reach. I used to sit on your shoulders to get up here. Lucky I'm tall these days. Taller than you ever were. But tall and heavy don't go well on a stack of red gum. I just touch the top of the light before the wood gives way and I have to jump clear. I've done it, though. I've knocked your spare key from the secret hiding place we made years ago. I have a way into your house.

The key turns smoothly despite not being used for at least sixteen months. The door swings inwards, asking me to come in. I take a step inside and close it behind me.

It's so quiet.

Janet has only been gone for two hours but I can feel the house lonely around me. I'm standing in the laundry and I can see the marks where the washing machine and the second fridge used to be. One fat fly zooms around the empty space. I step into the house properly, ignore your room on the left, walk into the kitchen. Everything smells lemony clean and I can almost see Janet scrubbing at the old benches, polishing the house so that it's ready for its new family. She's scrubbed away its history so the house, like her, can start again.

I go into Taylor's room, then Janet's, then the lounge. The carpet has been cleaned – it smells a bit steamy and when I touch it, it's still damp. One good cleaning that manages to take away every trace of who used to live here. The walls are clean too, more scrubbing.

What did she do to *your* room?

I stand very still. The roof creaks in the sun. The fly has followed me and circles my head until I smash it against the wall with a lightning-fast forehand swat. I can't feel you out here, Josh.

What did she do to your *room*?

I find myself in there without remembering how. I don't realize I've been holding my breath until it comes out in a noisy blast. Your room is empty, yes, but not clean. The carpet hasn't even been vacuumed. Fluff lines the wall where it meets the floor. Poster tack dots the walls. The curtains are half open like you left them. It smells, I'm not sure what of, but not the cleaning stuff that Janet used for the other rooms. Does it smell of you still? I don't know. It isn't strong enough to work it out.

I feel like I've walked to the South Pole. My legs are doing the wobbly thing. My breath is fast and I'm feeling a bit dizzy. It's easy to sink to the floor, crawl to the corner of your room behind your door where you used to throw your school bag, lean back against the cool plaster and prop my elbows on my knees.

Down here at ground level, the room seems lighter. I can see the dust speared by the sunbeams through the window. When I don't move for a while, the whirling dust slows down, travelling peacefully on the light to wherever dust goes.

I haven't been in your room since you were alive but I don't have any problem remembering what it was like. In the last six months of your life, you'd put photos of Bonnie up on your wall but besides that, things were the same as they had been for years. I'd spent so many days with you – so much of my life - I almost thought of this room as mine as well. I felt more like your brother than Taylor and not your little cousin because Taylor was always going to go and I wasn't ready to go yet. But you left me and now this room is someone else's. That unknown mystery family won't care. They'll remove the very last trace of you once they move in. You'll be out of here forever.

I sit and feel the hard wall behind my back and wait.

What am I waiting for? Your ghost? There are no such things as ghosts or I would have seen you before today. When you arrive in my nightmares I know that it's my imagination that put you there. Your soul has moved on, your body all but broken up into molecules. I'm not stupid, I know what happens when people die. There are no ghosts.

I put my hands either side of me and feel the gritty carpet. It's old, like the rest of the house, and sheds a bit under my hand. Yours is the worst room in the house. The carpet is rolled, stretched and saggy enough to make hills that we tripped over sometimes in our hurry to get in or get out. It's lumpy here under my hand.

Lumpy? In the corner of the room, the carpet is raised like there's something under it. I lean down, feeling around the edge of the carpet and lift the very corner. It peels back easily like a ripe banana skin. I see a book wedged there, a notebook opened in half by its spiral back and face down on the floorboards. I tug it out, let the carpet flop back and sit up to look.

Something about the notebook looks familiar although I know I've never seen it before. When I flick through it - fast because it's like I'm doing something I shouldn't - I see that most of its pages have something on them. Photos. Newspaper articles. Heaps of writing, your worst, some of it pressed so hard into the page that the ink comes through the paper. I don't read anything, I don't stop, but flick right through to the last page where you've written 'The End' like it was some cheap old paperback novel. I let the note-book slam shut.

What is this, Josh?

You kept a diary? But you could barely write!

You didn't read much either, except that book that Taylor had with the pictures you wouldn't show me because you said that I was too young.

You didn't keep anything for its sentimental value

although lots of stuff stayed in your room because you couldn't be bothered cleaning it up.

I close the book and put in on the floor while I feel around every inch of your carpet for anything else hidden under it. I don't find anything. I open your wardrobe and run my fingers along the panelling, testing for gaps or spaces where stuff could be wedged. Nothing. One notebook is all that remains in this room of you.

A door bangs - the front flyscreen in the wind. It scares the shit out of me. I move quickly around your room, looking behind the curtains, knocking the light shade to see if anything falls off and checking the plaster for hidden holes. Nothing, nothing, nothing. I scoop up the notebook and clutch it tightly. Now I'm sweating and it seems like a good idea to go. One last look. It's a lost room without you. It's a lost world without you. I back out, run through the house to the laundry door and go out into the stark summer day. I lock the door and balance the key back on the light by standing on that firewood again. I even restack the red gum.

No one will ever know - except me - that I've been to your house. That feels very sad and I wish now that I'd gone in yesterday when Janet was here. She is the one that would've understood this total realisation the most.

You are gone.

Full stop.

I walk away from your place feeling something drop from me. A little bit of extra weight that I've been carrying, something that pressed on my shoulders and my back and my heart that was squashing me. I realize that I've just been to a no-go zone. It should make me feel better, not having the fear of visiting your room on me. Instead, I wonder whether the weight that's pressing on me is actually holding me to the ground. Without it, I might fly away.

You didn't fly, you fell and died instead. Is that what will happen to me as well?

I start to run, scaling myself up like that tricky first bar. Immediately, heat pounds in my head. I go faster to catch up with it. I see someone in their front yard, venturing out of their house to get the mail. He stares at me like he can't believe what he's seeing. The heat makes the inside of my head red and I see you on the ground again, smashed on the ground under the tree, lying in such a strange way that I knew, even before I started screaming, that you were dead because no one could lie like that and still be alive.

When I can't go any faster, when my body gives out, I stop altogether and steal some water from someone's tap, splashing it over my face until I feel the heat ease. I play some music in my head (the soothing number 21) until my blood settles too and walk on to school.

I'VE BEEN so quick that I have to wait at Sofie's school, feeling uneasy, for her bell to go. We travel home and Dad's already there. 'Come to the pool?' he says to us.

'I don't need my whole family taking me to the pool,' Ella protests.

'I'll drive,' says Dad, grinning.

'Okay, then.' Ella goes to help Sofie find her things.

I take your notebook from my bag before we go and slide it under my mattress.

It's not bad when Dad goes to the pool with us. He loves the water and stays in longer than anyone else. His favourite thing to do is to float on his back with his eyes closed. For a big bloke, he floats really well. Actually, that's the reason he floats well – it's his fat holding him up. Sofie climbs on and he rolls over lazily to dunk her then ducks down to put her on his shoulders. She rises out of the water like a triumphant goddess, balanced easily. Her smile is bigger than the whole pool.

When I was smaller, he used to be able to throw me across the water. I'd shoot out, flung from his hands as he lifted me, and fly. He can't do it anymore – it would be like tossing a whale – so I watch him throw Ella. She's still skinny and zooms out of the water like a torpedo. Pool water falls in a dribbly arc around her.

'Is that your Dad?' Kendo flops down beside me. He's dripping and shakes his head to get the water out of his hair, leaving me covered in drops.

'Yeah.'

'Thought so. I know your sister. She's a friend of *my* sister's.'

'Is she?' I think of all the Year 7 girls that hang out together, a great mob of them looking pretty much the same. I only know the ones that El went to primary school with. I guess I haven't kept up much since then.

'Lewis in hospital?' Kendo stretches out on his stomach.

'Yeah.' A flicker of something runs through me. Worry? Panic? I still haven't heard from him. 'He'll be back in the next day or two.' I say that to reassure myself.

Kendo nods. 'You going home soon?'

I look at Dad, floating again. Sofie and Ella dive under him like he's a bridge. 'Doesn't look like it.'

Kendo pulls himself up. 'Well, I gotta go. See you at school.'

I take another look at comfortable Dad. I think how long he might be there. I think of your notebook and how it's a trace of you that I haven't finished exploring. 'Wait,' I say. 'I'll come with you.' I go to the edge of the pool. 'Dad! I'm walking home with Kendo.'

Dad waves lazily, a dugong flapping his flipper.

We walk out with our towels around our necks and start down the hill. 'It's so bloody hot this summer,' Kendo says, 'that we should live at the pool.'

'Except when it's raining.'

'What?'

I roll my eyes at him. 'It'd be okay living at the pool except when it's raining. And it's done that a lot this summer as well.'

'Yeah. You're right. Too wet. Well, I'll see you tomorrow.'

Kendo turns off to his place, leaving me to walk alone. The sun is shining right in my eyes so I walk watching the footpath. I don't see until I'm home that the driveway is empty, meaning that Mum's gone out and I've got the house to myself.

Instead of going straight to your notebook, though, I head for the piano. It's a magnet. Every time I walk through the lounge, it draws me in. The old thing needs a tune but I don't really mind. It talks with its own voice. Mum says that Great-Grandma played like a concert pianist – maybe it talks with *her* voice. She used to play at the movie theatre in the days before they had sound. Her music was the background to the film. They say that even when the film stopped, she kept on playing and that people could hear her music as they walked down the street and home. I guess she just liked it. Or maybe, like me, she thought that there was no movie if there wasn't any music and she wanted to keep the magic going. Or maybe she liked the sound of the piano echoing around the dark theatre even if she was the only one left to appreciate it.

I have another go at the étude, the first six bars, glancing once or twice into the shadow that is my room. I'm not sure what I'm putting off. What will I see if I go through your notebook again? I already know the end of your story.

The music is getting better, I can hear it myself. I try for another two bars. I play faster and louder until my fingers fall flat and the notes clang. I can almost hear Great-Grandma's disapproval. Quickly, I play something I know I can do really well - *Fur Elise* - to appease her. It might be Beethoven but it's an okay piece.

It finishes, *morendo*. I take a breath, push myself up, and brace myself for the task ahead. My heart is strangely pizzicato.

14

LEWIS

'Right,' says Tori. 'You're ready to go home.'

About time, too late, toll has been taken, I think.

'Great,' I say.

My bag takes no time at all to pack. The sketchbook fits snugly on top. On the way out, I see the sobbing boy's empty bed. He got taken away in the middle of the night by quick footed nurses and a running doctor. The rest of us weren't meant to hear but the code wasn't shut off quick enough. I feel bad. I didn't even find out his name and so the sobbing boy will always be *the sobbing boy*, a blue boy with grey eyes and a face washed with tears. I get the guilts for not trying harder to be kind or even play computer games with him but it's a dog eat dog world. I heard that phrase years ago on television. I *get* it, probably better than most. In some situations, it's every man for himself. That's how hospital makes me feel. Sorry, sobbing boy. It's a dog eat dog world.

The Judge is signing discharge papers or something. She glances up at me, looks that I've got my bag. She can't help herself – she has to go into my room and check that nothing has been left behind. For the first few days after I've been in hospital, she reverts to being a toddler's mum. Checking on me, checking me out, checking out everything I do. It'll pass. I hope I don't say anything cruel in the meantime.

The doctor bails me up before I reach the door to freedom. It's Ravi again. I see a new junior doctor every time I'm here and I know that Ravi won't be around the next time I come in. Dr Nightingale seems to be the only one who is always here. Dr Nightingale is not related to Florence Nightingale - the famous nurse from the Crimean War - but he seems to have been around for as long.

Dr Nightingale saw me yesterday on ward round. He has a heavy frowning face but also this sort of gentleness about him. 'Good lad, you're going well, good lad.' He always pats my hand before he goes away. I think Dr Nightingale is a bit of a legend. I'm not so sure about Ravi.

Ravi says, 'You understand everything, Lewis?'

I nod.

'Take care, then.' Ravi holds out his hand and I take it. He has a firm handshake. It's like a vote of confidence in me. Maybe he isn't so bad. My face cracks into a small smile.

The drive home takes just three hours, a bit more if you count the compulsory coffee break for Mum. Even though the traffic is flowing, the road is busy for some reason so Mum doesn't talk much but keeps her eyes on the road 'watching out for goddamnuselesshoons.'

I'm happy with her concentrating on other things beside me. I plug in my earbuds and listen to Pinpricks. Their music is loud and fills my eardrums with just the sort of thudding that clears my mind. When I feel like it, hours down the road, I take my phone out and turn it on for the first time in days. Bull's been texting. No one else.

At home, I go to my room and collapse on my bed, exhausted, probably because of the sobbing boy's midnight tricks. Mum must be tired too because she flicks the TV on and settles into one of her favourite long and romantically sad movies. The sickly-sweet music seeps under my door in a pink wave but I don't care. It's one of those home noises that somehow makes me feel better.

Dad comes in from work. I hear his keys on the kitchen bench and then he comes straight to me. 'Hello, Lewis. Okay then?'

'Good, Dad.' I wave my foot at him to show him my new, clean bandage. 'Nearly better.'

We don't have codes, Dad and I. He needs it straight. 'You mean, your sugar's okay too?'

'Pretty good. I just have to be careful while I'm on the antibiotics. I'll go and see Dr James next week.'

He nods, satisfied, and steps into the room to put one hand on my leg. 'Good to have you home.' He leaves, pulling my door shut.

That's a huge sign of affection coming from my old man. My leg tingles with it until Mum calls me for tea. We sit around the table with our plastic place mats and ex-peanut butter jar glasses and eat chicken kebabs without talking and I am so, so glad to be home. Everything seems bathed in rose.

15

BULL

R ight, Josh, I'm going in.
I balance the notebook on my knees. I am the last one to touch it since you did.

I try and slow my heart rate then before I notice I'm doing it, I plunge in, breath held as if I'm going into the diving pool.

Page one. It's a neatly cut-out newspaper article about a local politician's policy on the environment. It doesn't make sense that you would have put this in here. The only thing you thought about the environment is that when global warming arrives, it'll be pool weather for 9/10ths of the year. I look more carefully at the article but there's nothing mysterious about it. The date is January 28th of last year. The only thing that I can think of is that the date was ten months exactly to when you died.

Page two. Another newspaper article, this time of an Australian tennis player who just made it into the top ten. I fight the urge to yawn. I don't get your obsession with sport, especially as you didn't play any yourself. Yeah, you were fit, running for kilometres every day, but you were too small for football and too slow for tennis. You started to run with the Telford Track team but you preferred to run alone. I came with you sometimes – on my bike, though. You didn't like it much because I kept moving my wheels into your space. You liked the long bush tracks where no one else went so the old hut was a perfect hideaway for an hour or two of peace. There were times, though, when it wasn't peace you were after. On those days, you just ran and ran and ran.

Catch me!

I don't know whether you were running to something or running *from* something.

I come back to the present and flip through pages three, four, five, six. Predictable. More sports stars, a ticket stub from the Australian Open, a flyer for a demonstration match between two league teams that came to Telford.

Page seven, eight, nine, ten, eleven, twelve. You enter dark territory. Pages of heavy writing that I can't read. Pages of black, done in Texta. I imagined how you were feeling when you were deep in the hole that you fell into sometimes. I always pictured it with sides too high to climb out. You thinking that there was no hope of getting out.

A headache starts in my temples.

Page thirteen and there's a photo. A young man in uniform. His slouch hat sits carefully to one side of his head and his smile is wide and toothy. If I had to guess, I'd say he was just old enough to join the army and then only if he stretched the truth. The photo is in that old-fashioned sepia colour. It's fading and his face is nearly as pale as the background. I stare at him. There's something familiar about the shape of his nose, and the look on his face. That smile's so big it nearly swallows the rest of him. You've outlined the edges of the photo in the same thick, black Texta.

I peel the soldier off the page and the photo comes away with a bit of paper attached. I think there might be something written on the back of it but there's nothing there.

The door slams. I listen to see who it is. When there's the clink of car keys and the thud of shopping on the bench, I know it's Mum. I look back at the photo and a faraway thought arrives into my head. Mum will know who this is. I go into the kitchen.

'Will.' Mum jumps when she sees me. 'I thought you were at the pool with the others.'

'I walked home with Kendo.'

She nods then says, 'Are you okay, darling? You're so pale.'

I touch my face automatically, as if you can feel colour. 'I'm fine.' I go to back away but remember what I came to ask her. 'Do you know who this is?' I thrust the photo forward.

Mum takes it from me and turns to put it towards the light. She stares at it for a long time so I go and look over her shoulder. 'It's Uncle Len,' she says finally.

'Who?'

'My Uncle Len. Your Great-uncle Len. Grandpa's brother.'

'I don't remember an Uncle Len.'

'No.' Mum sighs. 'He died before you were born.'

I take the photo from her and look at it more closely. He doesn't look anything like how I remember Grandpa despite the obvious age difference. Photos seem different from that time, sort of washed out. Plus the fact that he's wearing a slouch hat. I couldn't see anyone I know in a slouch hat. 'Did he die in the war then?'

'No.' Mum moves to her shopping bags and starts to unpack. 'It was later.'

'Did Grandpa have any other brothers or sisters?'

'Only Len. They were very close.' Mum sighs again or maybe it's the plastic rustle of the banana bag.

I look across the kitchen and through the doorway to the lounge. It's too far away but I can just see the outline of a photo frame sitting on the sideboard. I know it's Grandpa, one of the last photos of him. He's sitting on his outside chair, an oversized zucchini in his arms. The look on his face is faintly puzzled as if he can't understand how the vegetable got so big. Grandpa died early in the year Sofie was born because I remember how sad Mum was that he would never see her.

The other photos on the sideboard are mainly us. 'I've never seen a photo of Uncle Len before.'

'Where did you get it?' Mum stops her unpacking and looks at me.

I hesitate then say truthfully, 'It was in Josh's stuff.'

'Oh.'

Then she's quiet for so long, I have to say, 'What's the matter?'

'Nothing,' she says but doesn't start unpacking again. 'It's just that there aren't many photos of Len left.'

I look at the soldier and feel sad. Once your photo was gone, were you forgotten?

'Will?' Mum says. 'Put it away for now.'

There's something strange about her voice that makes me say straight away 'Okay, Mum' but think 'No way. What's going on?' but I turn around and leave the kitchen to put the photo back in your notebook.

The front door swings open as I go past it. Sofie flies in, wet hair flapping around her face, followed closely by Ella and then Dad carrying all their stuff. His hair is tight wet curls on his head and he's grinning like he's just had the time of his life. I can't help smiling back. Dad's a simple bloke, Mum reckons. She says he just lives for the moment. Sometimes she says that with a smile but most of the time she looks annoyed as if Dad shouldn't be so bloody happy all the time. Maybe he should be looking to the future a bit more instead of plain-old enjoying the present.

I go to my room via the piano, giving the Chopin another ten minutes. I push myself to eight bars before crashing out badly and bolting to my room in disgust, automatically turning on my music player (it starts on number 30). I put Len away by sliding him half into my book shelf so that I can see the photo only if I'm lying on my bed. His smile is about all I can make out in the dying light of the day. I flick through the rest of your notebook but the photo of Great-uncle Len has taken up my brain space and I can't be bothered trying to decipher the loads of scribble you'd written. I close the book and push it into the gap where my mattress meets the bed frame on the side facing the wall. It sits snugly in there and won't be seen by anyone, especially as I make my own bed these days.

We eat dinner quietly. The week has tired us out. That, and the heat. The air-conditioner in the lounge makes a weak attempt to keep the rest of the house cool but we know it doesn't reach further than the couch. Dad put ceiling fans in all of the bedrooms and that's what we get to keep us cool. I like the feeling of air swishing past my skin and leave the fan on for most of the year, hot or not. The dining room must be the hottest room in the house but we always eat dinner in there. I watch as sweat trickles down Dad's forehead. He flicks it away and keeps eating his ham and salad. I wish it would rain. It's always better after some rain.

When Mum goes into the kitchen to make herself a cup of tea (as she always does, summer or winter) and the girls leave to watch their stupid Friday night TV shows, I lean across to Dad.

'Dad?'

'Yeah?' He takes another slice of bread and folds it into four before cramming it into his mouth.

'Did you know Mum's Uncle Len?'

Dad nods without speaking. When he swallows, he says, 'I went fishing with him a few times.'

'What happened to him?'

Dad turns to me. 'Why do you want to know?'

I shrug. 'I didn't even know I had a Great-uncle Len.'

'Hmm,' says Dad.

'Well?'

'He died.'

'Yeah, well, no kidding.'

'He died in a car accident.'

I nod. Sad.

Dad leans forward. 'It was a single car accident.'

'Kangaroo, maybe?'

'No, mate.' Dad looks at me for a moment, trying to work something out. Finally, he makes a decision. 'Len used to drive his car too fast sometimes. He was a wild sort of bloke. One day he ran the car into a tree.'

I sit very still. 'You mean…'

'We don't really know what happened. Sometimes he was a really strange man and the things he did didn't make much bloody sense.' Dad suddenly looks upset. 'Don't tell your mother I told you, okay? It was a rotten thing for the family. Your grandpa was beside himself. I don't think he ever recovered properly.' Dad's face twists with the pain of it. 'Even though he was the one who had to deal with his moods, Grandpa thought the world of Len.'

I nod, something in the back of my mind refusing to take shape.

'Will?' calls Mum from the kitchen. 'Bring those plates up.'

I stand and stack and walk into the kitchen and load the dishwasher and go to walk away.

'You alright?' Mum says after me.

'I think I ate too much,' I say with a fake groan and a rub of the stomach.

In my room, I stand directly under the ceiling fan and have a think. Something is blocked in my head and it takes me a while to work it out. I see my school bag on the chair and take my science folder out. The genogram is stuck in a plastic pocket in the front. I pull it out. Mum's side is still blank but I start to fill it in. Mum and Janet, only daughters of Grandpa (Thomas) and Gram (May). There doesn't seem to be a spot for Len but I add him in. Then I put Ella and Sofie next to me, and you and Taylor under Janet and your disappearing alcoholic dad Rory. I stop and take a good look. Len's name seems to stand out.

Dad said that Len had moods. Len sounds a bit like you. Grandpa didn't ever recover from Len's death – maybe I'm a bit like him. So we're all related, in a tragic way. I stare at the genogram, wondering what else there is that ties us all together.

16

LEWIS

rt Draws Alec to the City
Headline, page three, City News. There's an article about this fifteen-year-old boy who came to the city just for the class from the back blocks of a small country town. There's a picture of the kid wearing a checked windcheater, hair over his face and jeans torn at one knee. He isn't smiling. Sam Keally stands behind him, wearing a wide grin and holding a Keally sketchbook open in one hand. Maybe it's the kid's. Further in the background are a gang of oldies sitting at desks. Everyone is smiling but the country boy.

I can't believe that this kid stole the limelight. He looks like a dick. I'm so glad that it wasn't my photo in the paper looking like that with Sam Keally. The article doesn't even say that the kid could draw, only that he was fifteen and travelled all the way to the city. Like no one else does that for lots of other reasons. Going into hospital, for example.

I shut the paper and fold it into four ready for the recycling bin. I throw it on the floor on top of a pile of clothes and lie back on my bed. I had come into my room to sketch but Mum had followed me in with the paper. For some reason, she thought I'd like to see it. From this angle, my ceiling is a clear yellow. Maybe it's the evening summer sunlight or maybe it's the rage in my eyes. Whatever, it's like the old Indian yellow, peoli, gogili, snowshoe yellow that I saw once in a book. This pigment was originally from the urine of cows that had been fed exclusively on mango leaves. The cows died eventually, but their contribution to art was something that has never been fully replicated in the synthetic world.

I remember reading that and thinking, humans are cruel bastards.

Newspaper ink used to be toxic if you inhaled it but it was alright once it was dry on the page. I catch myself on the verge of thinking that it would be fantastic if newspaper print poisoned those in newspaper pictures and realize that I really need to get out of the house. I haul myself upright and go outside into the bright bright day.

I've been inside too long and forgotten the intensity of the sun. If I had any sense, or had been wearing my bathers, I would have gone straight to the pool but I don't have either so I keep walking. I should be going to see Bull but I don't want to see anyone at the moment. Then as soon as I think that, I turn the corner and there are Bonnie and Jordan together under trees in the park.

They're too far away to be aware of me. They're too busy to be aware of me. I stare - can't stop myself. Jordan has his bulk half on top of Bon and his elbows either side of her head. They're kissing like there's no tomorrow but I see Bonnie bend her knee up and use her foot to shift her body just a bit away so Jordan slides mostly off her. Her hands are under his arms and around his back and it doesn't look like she's trapped, just held down. I keep walking because if I stop they will notice me. The path takes me closer to them than I would like.

I walk past.

I hear Bonnie say, 'No.'

I slow down.

She doesn't say anymore.

The path takes me around the edge of the park and it's not until I go around the corner and half way up the block before I can see them again. Jordan is sitting up, one elbow on his knee, looking into the park. Bonnie is still lying down but as I watch, she sits then stands and starts brushing at her T-shirt and shorts. Her fingers comb her hair. Jordan is still looking towards the kid's playground although it's too hot for anyone to be on it and Bonnie stops still. I think she's waiting for him to say something. He stares on, speechless.

My legs have carried me onwards, past the beautiful Bonnie and her arrogant pig of a boyfriend.

If I had a toxic cow right then, I'd command it to piss on him. A bright yellow Jordan would be the only one worth seeing.

17

BULL

I get a text on Saturday from Lewis.
C u @ 11. Mall.
It's 8.30. I'm not up yet.
OK.
U up?
No. Piss off.
Lazy bastard
Yeah

I roll onto my stomach with my hand touching the carpet, letting my phone drop. The genogram I started the night before is right under my nose. I pick up a pen and run a few more lines out for Great Grandma the concert pianist and her farmer husband.

When Lewis doesn't text me back, I get dressed and raid the kitchen. No one else is around. I guess that Mum is already out doing the things she doesn't get time to do during the week. *Haircut 8.00am*, I see written on the calendar. Mum never sleeps in. She's the last one to bed, the first one up. I lean back against the bench while I wait for toast to cook. The kitchen is bald. No dishes in the sink. Two tea-towels folded in half hang from the oven door. The floor is shiny – maybe she mopped it before she went out. The toast pops. I spread thick margarine and pile the jam on. From the corner of my eye I see the clothes line full of washing, hanging limp in the already-hot morning sun.

By 9.30 I'm on my bike, heading for the Mall. Lewis said 11.00 but I can't stay at home any longer. The walls are closing in on me. I can't play the piano or the guitar because Dad's still asleep. My fingers feel itchy so I leave home.

I roll into the bike racks near the library and make my way to Muso's World. Some guys are hanging out around the guitars so I go into the sheet music section and have a look. Most of it is stuff for teachers and music students but every now and then I discover treasure. Last time I looked I got REM's PVG book for half price because the cover was torn. Today, the pickings are not ripe. I pull out a book of Chopin's polonaises because his picture on the front cover catches my eye. He looks stern and unhappy but he shouldn't be. He *should* look noble to match his Polish music, but not sad. What's he got to be sad about? People are still talking about him 200 years after he died.

'Chopin?'

The voice makes me jump. I look up into Grace's smiling face. I swallow. She is so intensely beautiful.

'Yeah,' I say, trying to think. 'I've got this thing for old dead guys.'

'Right,' she says, angling her head so I can see the full hoop of earring on her right ear. Her earlobe pulls down a bit with its weight – I've never noticed. There's a dark mark on her neck but it's not what I think it is as first. It's another tattoo, a faded spider. It grips her neck like it's not letting go.

Grace turns slightly and I see Bonnie standing behind her. My face falls like molten lead.

'What are you here for?' I say, talking to Bonnie but looking at Grace.

'I'm getting a music stand for my brother's birthday,' says Grace. 'He plays guitar.'

'Does he? I don't know him.'

'He's only in Grade 3. He doesn't go to our school.'

I shrug, embarrassed. 'There you go, then.'

Grace turns away to get the stand, her arm just touching mine as she goes. Bonnie stays where she is. I try to forget she's there and flip through the polonaises to the back of the book. There're some quotes from Chopin. I read to myself.

"…inside something gnaws at me;

some presentiment, anxiety, dreams – or sleeplessness –
melancholy, indifference –

desire for life, and the next instant, desire for death;

some kind of sweat peace, some kind of numbness, absent-mindedness…"

I close the book and put it back.

Bonnie's still there. I try to think of something to say to her but I just can't. I feel the stress of our last conversation close over me like a trap. Anyway, she could say something to me, couldn't she? She's looking as if something's stopping her, too. Maybe I should show her what Chopin wrote? Would she understand sleeplessness, anxiety, desire? I feel a little tremor go through me and I have to turn away. I can't deal with Bonnie, I can't. Her pain is as sharp as mine and so we're just two razor blades stabbing each other.

I walk away and go over to the guitars. Some idiot is trying to play *Swing Temple* (number eight). His friends laugh. I'm tempted to pull the guitar right off him and show him how it's done but instead I grin along with the rest of them.

From the corner of my eye, I see Grace and Bonnie leave, the music stand in its bag swinging from Grace's hand. Her fingernails are painted fluorescent green and match her orange swirling dress in a psychedelically weird way. I realize that every little thing about her makes me like her more and I suddenly love green nail polish. I wish she'd come in without Bonnie. Maybe we could have hung around together? Now that's one of the stupidest thoughts I'd ever had.

Grace pauses at the window, sees me, lifts a hand, tilts her head. Then she disappears around the corner, Converses flashing, head bent towards Bonnie's. I turn back to the guitar dudes, feeling stunned.

Muso's World is a great shop. They don't mind if you play the instruments. They *want* you to play the instruments. It gets the shop noticed. Sometimes I've been in here when real musicians have been playing. You know, the people that have that genius touch and music pours from them like it's a language only they know. I'm not bad at what I play, pretty good really when I think about it, but I have to work hard. Music flows from me like heavy treacle. Slowly and thickly. I'm no genius. I wish I was.

I think Chopin was a genius. And Mozart, Beethoven, Liszt. Maybe it was easier being a genius back then. Maybe it was encouraged and not seen as a freaky thing like it might be these days. Chopin started composing when he was six, and played in his first big concert at eight. He outgrew his music teachers and didn't have any lessons for years. He didn't seem to need them. He was just *musical*. He must have been born that way. How much harder was it for Cobain being born in today-land instead of yesterday-land?

I wander away from the guitars to the pianos. I'm still thinking of Chopin when I start playing so a little bit of that chromatic étude comes out. I try to imagine how it must have been for him having all those notes galloping around in his head the whole time and wonder if it was a relief to get them down on paper. I play those first eight bars I've been practicing then my memory fizzles out. I play them again, faster. Then again. I look up to see one of the guitar guys listening. 'That was good, mate,' he says.

I shake my head. No it wasn't because I stumbled in the fifth, so this guy doesn't know a thing about music.

'Yeah, real good. Wish I played.' His turn to shake his head, but sadly.

'You just have to do it, mate.'

'Nuh, can't,' he says.

I shrug. Yeah he can. 'You have to work at it.' He just can't be stuffed trying. I know the sort of guy he is. Wants it to be easy, to be instant.

Like you and that night you played and played and played and your fingers bled all over the strings.

'You all right?' The guitar guy is looking at me as if I've suddenly got boils all over my face. 'You're shaking.'

'Had food poisoning last night,' I manage to squeak, feeling like my body is shutting down. 'I'm still sick. I'd better go.'

Somehow, I get out of the shop and into the hot but fresh air. I make myself walk through the Mall, hands in pockets, head down as if I'm late for an appointment. Inside my head, I'm muttering. *I hate you, Josh. Hate you. I'm so mixed up because of you.*

I breathe in and out as I walk, concentrating on the slap of my feet on the pavers. Step, step, breath in, step, step, breathe out. I go the whole length of the Mall before I stop seeing double and then turn and come the whole length back before I can put my head up and look at the crowds. I can't see Grace but wish I could. I wish I could tell her about how I just lose it sometimes remembering you. I think she'd know what to say to me. Grace, though, is nowhere to be seen. I go to a café I've never been to before and order an iced coffee then sit in the very back corner to wait for Lewis.

At five to eleven, I text him to say where I am. He comes in a few minutes later and I am so glad to see him that I punch him on the arm. He sits, angling his long legs under the table. He has that pale hospital look that he gets when he's been away, no matter how long he's in for. Don't they let patients out into the sunshine? How can it be good for people to be locked up?

'Lew,' I say.

'Bull,' he says. 'Have I missed anything?'

I think: Janet's gone. I broke into her house like a desperate burglar. And I'm in love with Grace Fountain. 'Nuh,' I say. 'Lots of homework.'

'Been hot?' he says.

'Well, yeah,' I say.

'It's hard to tell…' he trails away then. 'What are you doing in here?'

I pick my glass up. 'Thirsty.'

Lewis grunts. 'Let's go to the art shop.'

I follow him out. We go past Muso's World and a new lot of guys are hanging around the guitars. 'I saw Grace in there,' I say because I can't help it. I leave Bonnie out.

'Hope you were doing something cool at the time. Bass solo? Heavy metal?'

I shake my head. 'I was looking at a book on Chopin.'

Lewis raises his hands and lets them drop. 'Mate. Missed opportunity.'

We walk on.

'He had cystic fibrosis.'

'What?' I half turn to Lewis.

'Chopin.' Lewis shrugs. 'They used to say that he died of tuberculosis. Now they say he had cystic fibrosis.'

'What's that?'

Lewis doesn't answer straight away. 'It's a hereditary condition. You have it from birth.'

'How do you know that?'

This time, he turns to look at me. 'I just know.'

I nod. We walk on. He knows a lot of things, does Lewis. Things about diseases that he learnt in hospital and from keeping up with his own problems. Things I hope I never have to learn.

The art shop is nearly empty when we get there. They've got big comfy chairs to sit in. I slump in one and let Lewis browse. This shop is not like the music shop – they don't let you muck around with the goods.

Lewis spends ten minutes looking through sketch pads before he picks up a thick black-covered one that looks slightly different to the ones he usually gets. Maybe it's a different brand. He buys it with a twenty dollar note that The Judge must've given to him because Lew usually just deals in change scabbed from around his house. He tucks the book under his arm and we go out. I get my bike and walk it with him. We leave the Mall behind.

I guess I'm not thinking straight, glad to be out in the sun, glad that Lewis is back. We walk aimlessly around the back of the skate park and I'm watching the blurring spokes on my bike wheel, when I suddenly find myself at the park.

At that tree in the park.

It's a tall, thick, old tree with scribbly marks on it from burrowing grubs. I have been told it's a beautiful tree with its smooth white bark and its mellow green leaves. The tree might be but the area around it isn't. You went up that tree so fast it couldn't hold you.

Catch me, Bull!

When you hit the ground, that was the end of it. I didn't see you fall but I did see you lying broken on the ground. And the blood soaked dirt. And one shoe, torn off you as you fell, lying upside down against the trunk. There's nothing to see now, just dust and dead leaves.

'Bull?'

Lewis is yelling in my face but I can only just hear him. I know he's yelling because I see his mouth red and wide and the muscles straining his neck. He's so close that his head bangs mine when he shakes me. My head rings and his voice gets loud, as if someone's turned the volume to max.

'Bull!'

I push him away and he flies back, bum first onto the ground. I cover my ears with my hands to keep his noise out but he stands up again and pulls them away. This time I punch him with both fists. He dodges but not all the way. I catch him on the arm and he shouts in pain. His throw connects with my stomach. I double over, more in surprise than pain, and try to breathe. Slowly his voice – 'Bull, Bull, Bull you idiot' – slides back to normal. I stand up nearly all the way and look into his wide-eyed face.

'Let's go,' he says.

He drags me with his good arm, holding the other tucked into his side. I stumble off with him, still not quite straight, until we get to the other side of the park. He leaves me there on a bench and I sit hugging my stomach as he goes back and gets my bike. I watch as he wheels it slowly over and lowers it to the ground then sits beside me in silence.

After what seems like three days, I say, 'Sorry about that.'

He nods. We sit.

'It's that tree,' I say, another day later. 'I haven't been there…'

He nods again.

I have nothing left to say.

Eventually we leave, still without saying anything. As I turn into the driveway at home to get ready for work, I see that Lewis is clutching his sketchbook under one arm. Its black cover is covered in dust. I feel shame.

I GO to work shaky and tired, wondering how the day will end.

The very best of things and the very worst of things happen when I'm working. There was one shift when Kendo, Jake and I had absolutely nothing to do but make up combinations of hamburgers for ourselves. I had four meat patties, each layered with pickles, smothered in mustard and with maple syrup to finish off. Jake had a pile of chicken nuggets with hashies (pretty ordinary) but managed to squash flat six buns and put them in between the other layers. Bit doughy, really. But Kendo – he was the King of Self-Serve. He went to every food station and put everything he could between thick slices of processed cheese – stuff the bread, he said. In the end he had a sloppy mess of ice-cream and meat and tomato sauce. Watching him eat it made me gag but, hey, he was cool.

There were other shifts that made my heart sink and stay so low I thought it would never beat properly again. They would be when Michelle was doing her best to crush me, and Kendo wasn't around and I was feeling rock bottom to start with.

It makes me think about what I'm going to do when I leave school. If I get a job that makes me feel like Speedy Sam's Burgers, I'll sometimes be the happiest bloke around and sometimes the saddest. On the happy days everything would be alright. On the sad days, I'll be thinking that the rest of my life looks grim.

Today is one of those days when I shouldn't have gone to work. I came in feeling bad and left feeling worse. Michelle got me every chance she could, calling me Bull Burger like she'd discovered the best sort of insult.

'Hey, Bull Burger, hurry up with those chips.'

'Bull Burger, clean that bench top down.'

The other guys laughed when she first said it but even they got sick of it after an hour or two. Finally, Jack turned around and said, 'Shut up, Michelle. That's enough.'

Ordinarily that would get someone sacked on the spot. Abuse of Manager. Too bad that it started with Abuse of Kitchen Hand. But Michelle liked Jack, was probably in love with him. She looked up into his handsome brown eyes and said something lame like, 'Watch who you're speaking to, Jack Rodgers.' But Jack didn't give a shit. He just turned back to his work. We all did. I didn't even say thanks. I felt crappy for not being able to stand up for myself.

I finished right on four o'clock and went straight home. No one else was there. I sat at that piano with my fat-soaked hair and sweat running off my face and played for two hours straight. By the time the others got home I had the first page - fourteen bars - nearly under control but I was exhausted. Did I feel better? Maybe. It would have been hard to feel any worse.

18

LEWIS

'Josh was a bit full on.'

I'm not even going to try and guess what it would have been like to see your cousin dead on the dusty ground of a community park. Kendo and Charlie told me what happened but not for a couple of months after I'd been at school. I was already friends with Bull. I could see he was struggling with something big and I'd heard that Josh had died in an ugly way. I didn't know the details and really didn't want to know but I asked one too many questions. Kendo filled me in, with Charlie sad and serious in the background adding bits when Kendo paused.

'He didn't jump, he fell.'

'That tree, everyone climbed it. Josh was the only one who got up so far.'

'And fell.'

'Bull was running after him.'

'They say Bull was chasing him.'

'They say Josh was just running like he did sometimes.'

'They say Josh went up that tree laughing and shouting. Out of control. It was all over by the time Bull got there.'

'He found Josh at the bottom of the tree.'

'He found Josh already dead.'

I felt sick all afternoon.

By the end of last year, Bull seemed to get better. He laughed more, took on a solo in orchestra, handed in all his homework. The summer was fine, too. It was me who seemed to be struggling then, with doctor visits and crap like that. Maybe I took my eye off the Bull, so to speak. This last month, he doesn't seem so good, not since Janet sold the house.

The new sketchbook lies unopened on the bed in front of me. I finished the last page of the old one last night. I don't know. The new book is strange without its Keally brand, but I suddenly don't want to have anything to do with Sam Keally anymore. It can't really matter what sketchbook I have – they're all the same.

Another minute passes and I open the book. Its paper is acid free, 140gsm, same as the other. It should catch my drawings exactly the same. I run my hand over it testing its surface, then pick up my smudgy 9B. I start with the shadows, making darkness surround her, and then bring Bonnie out into the light. I should swap to something finer but I just concentrate on her shape rather than the detail. No one but me would know it is her.

'Hey, Lewis,' she had said to me the day before I went into hospital. 'What's the matter?'

I shrugged like an idiot.

She had stared at me for a while after that. Grace and Jules were behind her in the corridor, heads sharing earpieces. Everyone else was walking around, going some-where, doing something. I don't know where Bull was. Not there, though. It was as if Bonnie and I were alone in the world.

'Sometimes,' she said, dropping her voice so I had to lean forward to hear, 'I just got to get away from this.'

This. She meant the swirling place we were standing in.

'Where do you go?'

'I've got somewhere.' Her head bent towards mine.

Maybe she would have said more but the bell shrieked from the PA. The mass of students at the lockers started clanging them shut, yelling at each other, and scuffing along the corridor to classes. Grace loomed and Bonnie stood up straight. I saw the look on Grace's face as she switched her gaze from me to Bon. Her eyes were like laser beams shining into our brains. Bonnie turned away without saying anything more.

I make her hair long strokes of dark satin and touch the pencil to her eyes.

This 9B doesn't get used a lot. It's almost as long as the day I got it. I usually prefer colour so I'm sort of surprised that this drawing has worked so well. Must be the subject matter.

'Who's that?'

The book falls from my lap and slides across the doona. I pick it up. There's a long smudge where it dragged across my knee.

Mum looks aghast. 'I didn't mean to scare you.'

'Maybe you'd better knock next time. This *is* my room.'

My voice is hard. I see Mum's shock. I feel my shock.

'Sorry.' She turns and leaves, just like that.

How do you feel now, Lewis Pascoe?

Fine, actually.

Sometimes the pressure of being the only kid in this house overflows like this. She seems to always be there. That's not a fair thing to say, seeing as it's her house as much as mine, but I don't want her focus to be just on me. If Dad was around more, maybe things would be different but he seems to spend more time with Max than Mum. I look at my ruined picture, pick up the eraser and rub at it gently until I'm happy with it again.

Mum goes outside to get the washing. I can see the flap of sheets from where I'm sitting. I suddenly feel rotten for snapping at Mum. I feel rotten, too, about Bull and whatever it is that he's feeling about Josh that makes him freak out like he does.

I close the book on the gorgeous untouchable Bonnie, put the pencil away, and go to help Mum.

19

BULL

'Bye, bye, bye,' we said to Mum, Ella and Sofie at the door. They were off to see Aunt Janet again. 'Don't hurry back,' I said to myself as they drove off.

The boys have been left alone. You can feel the relief in the air. Dad is sprawled in his arm chair, asleep already in front of the cricket with an empty beer can rolling around on his guts. I'm playing *Battle Scar* on the computer because Mum never lets me when the girls are around and Dad wouldn't care even if he was awake. We go about our business for a couple of hours until lightning flashes right over the house and the power goes off. Dad snorts awake.

'Power's off,' I say.

'What?' I hear the can clank to the floor. 'Right.'

It's not dark outside but the house is glum. I go to the laundry and find a couple of head torches. Dad puts one on. I hold mine in my hand.

'Check this out, Dad.' I shine the light on my hand and make rabbit ears.

'Look at this.' His big hands make a barking dog.

We muck around for a bit shining spots around the place. Thunder bashes our ears from outside.

'You hungry?' says Dad. The glaring spotlight hides his head. He looks like a monster.

'Starving.'

'Let's go out. We can't do anything here for a while.'

Dad takes a while to find the car keys and his wallet. He whistles the whole time he's looking. I go and stand on the back step and watch the rain pelt down from the cover of the eave. Just as suddenly as it started, it stops, but the power stays off. We get in the car and drive to the club where Dad knows there's a generator.

We used to go out every Friday night when it was free meals for kids under twelve at the RSL. Once Ella turned thirteen, it meant that only one of us had a free meal and Dad realized he was paying a fortune to feed us. So we haven't been out for a while. I order the same thing that I always used to – Fisherman's Basket. Dad has steak and chips.

We're half way through our meals when I see Dad tense up, staring at something behind me. It's so unusual that I stop chewing, swallow and turn around to look. There's a man sitting alone on the table next to ours. I don't recognize him. He nods seriously at Dad. Dad nods back. He attacks his steak again.

'Who's that, Dad?' I whisper.

'Just someone I haven't seen for a while.'

'Who?'

'Eat your chips before I do.'

I slice a calamari ring in two and stuff it in my mouth. Dad glances over at the man every now and then. I start to do it too, sure that I should know him. We live in a reasonably small town but I guess I don't have to know everyone in it. I wonder if the other man feels us staring at him but when I take another quick look, he's eating happily and doesn't seem at all disturbed.

'We should do something tomorrow,' says Dad. 'You know, just us.'

'What do you want to do?'

Dad thinks. I think. We don't normally do stuff alone, there's never a chance. And it's not like I'm into sitting on the couch with him to watch the cricket. I realize that there's not a lot that Dad and I have in common. But a light goes on in Dad's head. 'We could come here.'

Huh? 'We're here already.'

'No, I mean tomorrow. See?' Dad points across at the notice board next to the menu on the wall. *The Frank Brothers,* says the flyer. *Direct from Tamworth.* 'A music band. We could come and see them.'

I look hard at Dad to see how much he's kidding but he isn't. Not at all. When I don't say anything, he says, 'Well, you're into music and that.'

'I'm not really into *country* music, Dad.' Nothing on my list is country.

'I don't think they're country.' Dad peers again at the flyer. 'Oh. *Direct from Tamworth Country Music Festival.* You could be right.'

'It's okay, Dad. I've got stuff to do at home. You probably have, too.'

'Yeah.' Dad finishes his steak and pushes his plate away. 'Yeah, I probably have.'

I roll my eyes at my crumbed prawns. You know, most of the time you wouldn't think Dad lived in the same house as me. I wonder how much he hears when I play the piano or the guitar or the gigantic double bass that takes up half of the spare room. Maybe it's just background noise to him, just one of many in a household full of kids. Chopin equals Slim Dusty equals Ella yelling equals Sofie giggling. Maybe that's why he's so happy all the time, he hears every household sound as the same and none of it worries him.

Someone's phone beeps. It's such a loud beep that I look around without thinking. The man behind us takes something from his belt and as he moves his arms, I glimpse his uniform. He looks at the pager and stands up. I see the whole of him tall against the table. He leaves quickly, his dinner going cold and his chair still out. I look back at Dad. He shrugs and looks down. 'Ambo,' he says.

I remember him.

He's one of the guys who came to you.

I flush hot and cold and feel my chips curl around in my stomach. He was the one that said you fell twenty-five metres, half the length of the pool. He said a branch caught you on the way down and speared you as you fell. It wasn't meant to happen, you were just climbing a tree. Trying to climb higher than anyone had ever climbed. You could do it in your manic state. It was a simple enough idea even though I knew it was stupid. The reason no one else had climbed any higher than the last thick, straight branch was that it was too hard to go any further. You had to go further.

I sat with you until the ambulance came and Dad pulled me away. I remember the ambo guy's face as they covered you up. He was white. Death-touched. He spoke to Dad at the time and maybe he spoke to Dad later, I don't know. Didn't he have a son the same age as you?

'Will?' Dad's calling me and the sights fade. I slowly come back to him. 'You alright?'

'Yeah, Dad,' someone says from a long way away. 'I'll be okay.'

We finish up and leave. Dad puts his arm around me as we walk out and it's as heavy as a log. It's raining slightly again and the mist on my face is good. Dad grips my shoulder just as we climb into the car. I think he does it for him as well as me. I keep forgetting that Dad had a rough time as well when you died. Maybe it catches up with him unexpectedly – making him shaky and sad - like it does to me. Seeing that ambo brought that day back for him, too.

After you died, when it was really hard to talk, Dad often took me for drives. We'd go out into the bush and along the pot-holed tracks that have been left to wash away since the gold rush. Riding those tracks would rattle the teeth from anyone's gums and Dad liked to take them hard. No one could get any words out being shaken like that and so it didn't matter if the words had left my body.

The other place we went to was the creek watch, not to drive over potholes but to stop and have a bit of thinking time. I had thought it was all for me but maybe Dad needed it as well. The creek watch is a flat area of nothing that overlooks Telford Creek. And Telford Creek isn't a babbling brook of a creek, it's an open drain that runs down the centre of a concrete culvert. When there's hardly any water, it looks like sludge and smells like rotting garbage. When it rains like this it races brown and frothy and has branches and supermarket trolleys caught up in the swirls. Lots of people come to the creek watch when it rains hard. You can watch the water rise until it laps at the edge of the ground where the cars are parked.

We drive to the creek watch. Ten other cars are there already so we have to park at the side. Dead shrubs block the view so I get out and stand at the edge, looking down into the water. It is an angry creek today. We've had lots of rain this week and the water levels have already been up. The creek has branches in it and a heap of plastic bags. No supermarket trolleys yet. Dad comes to stand next to me. The water creeps up the sides of the concrete.

Someone else shouts first but I see it at almost the same time. Head back, ears flattened, paws pushing against the water, a cat whirls past. The water is raging. The sides of the culvert are too steep here to be able to do anything but half a kilometre up, the concrete ends and weeds take over. A group of guys take off along the edge, running awkwardly in their bare feet and board shorts. Dad and I, and the rest of the people on the creek watch, follow them. Dad huffs and lumbers but I don't feel like going ahead of him. The guys are well in front. I see one of them jump over the edge into the weeds.

We get there just as it's all over. The cat is swooped up with the hero guy waist deep in brown water. It looks like he'll fall and go under but he must be gripping hard with his toes. His mates shimmy down the bank, linked together in a human chain, and pull him out. The cat looks pathetic and frightened, its black and white fur clumped and clinging to its body. One of the guys strips his shirt off and they wrap the cat up. The crowd huddles around them. Someone takes photos. I stand back and watch them. Lucky cat, I think. You are one hell of a lucky cat. Caught before you died.

We drive back home in silence. The storm is over for the time being and the power has come back on. Maybe it's all that food I ate but I don't feel so good, sort of irritable and twitchy. I leave Dad to settle back into his chair and go to my room. I sit in the semi-darkness for a while but I keep seeing the drenched cat and its struggle against the water. What if the hero guy had missed and the cat had kept going? It would have gone under and drowned.

It seems too easy to imagine how it would be to drown, to sink into blackness.

I flick my light on, grab the guitar and play a fierce turnover of four chords. The strings of this bass are my lifeline and I'm hanging on hard.

20

LEWIS

Wound healed. Energy levels charged. Life in balance. Yes, I'd never say this to anyone out loud in case I jinx myself but I feel better than I have for a long time. When I get up on Sunday, I smile so widely at Mum that she gives a spontaneously surprised grin back, as if it's been a long time since she's seen me so happy. I smile at Dad sitting at the breakfast table eating crumpets and reading a trashy Sunday paper. Dad sees and his eyebrows go up but he just keeps chewing. It makes me smile even more.

A text comes through. Charlie. *Bonnie & Jordan split. I gotta chance now.* Charlie's kidding – he wants Grace, not Bonnie. I text back. *No chance cos ur fugly.*

I go to my bedroom to think about this new bit of information. Bonnie had linked up with Jordan at the end of last year. Jordan is two years older, two years bigger. He went to Eagle Hill Secondary where he had the reputation of a predatory reptile. That reputation kept with him when he got his welding apprenticeship. Why had Bonnie gone out with him in the first place? I think I know – Jordan is a safe guy, big and tough and indestructible. The picture of health and predictability. Not fragile like Josh had ended up at the same age. Nothing like me, either.

I feel a pang of sympathy for Bonnie, that is, if Charlie's got it right. Charlie's usually right, though. He isn't one to make things up. You can trust him more than Kendo. I feel sad for Bonnie but happy for myself. Ecstatic, even. Maybe I'm still high from waking up feeling so bloody fantastic.

I draw Bonnie again in my sketchbook, this time in colour. I keep swapping pencils so that she comes out like a rainbow. I give her ultramarine eyes, even though hers are brown. She keeps her hair swept over one eye so that she has to hold it back to see you properly. I draw her with her hair down, how she wants it to be, but make it spectrum orange. She's in a super hero victory stance, one foot on the writhing body of Jordan. Her arms are crossed, satisfied. That's how you should be feeling, I think, before giving her a gold Viking helmet. Got rid of that poisonous snake before he could do you any harm.

———

I PUT the book down and text Bull the news. Charlie wouldn't have done it. He knows Bull doesn't talk to Bonnie and that she's an out-of-bounds subject. Bull doesn't text back but I'm not surprised. He'll read the message when he's ready. I think that he'll feel a bit better about Bonnie after this. Maybe feeling better about Bonnie will make him feel better about himself. Maybe then he'll let Josh go and start to live properly again.

I feel so good I head to the carpet and do fifteen push-ups, the blood pumping through my arms and making them swell. I flip over and crunch until I'm nearly winded. When I flop back on the floor, stretched out long and mean, I smile idiotically at the ceiling. I'm feeling pretty superhuman myself.

21

BULL

Monday morning. When I swing out of bed, I stand on the genogram. 'Shit.' I need to hand it in.

I grab the paper off the floor and study it. I'm not sure what to do but it seems to me to be unfinished business. Uncle Len's photo is a shadow on my bookshelf and although I'm not looking at it, I see it sitting dark and mysterious. I fold the genogram in four and put it in my school bag.

My phone comes off its charger and I turn it on. It bleeps with a message from Lewis. *News from Charlie. Bonnie & Jordan split.*

I frown, and wait to feel happy. Bonnie should never have gone with Jordan and now it's over. I'm not happy, though. I just feel confused.

I don't give a rat's arse.

This is what I'd like to send to Lew but decide not to answer at all.

I was yelling at Bonnie about Jordan and now she's not going out with him but I still feel like yelling at her. Maybe it's just that I feel like yelling? The thought worries me and

I decide to be as quiet as I can in case the yelling starts and won't stop. I take Sofie to school without saying anything and she looks at me, puzzled, as she turns to go in.

'Have a good day, Sofie,' I whisper. 'Learn something.'

She smiles, a tiny one only, and goes into school.

The relentless summer heat has given us a break for the day, with the top temperature only expected to be 31 degrees. Bloody ice age coming. When I get to the classroom, though, the smell of sweat still hangs in the room. It'll take a winter to get rid of that.

Casual day today, no uniform. Lewis swans in with a jumper on. What. An. Idiot.

'Give it a break, Lew!'

'What?'

Kendo walks behind him, muscle shirt doing its job nicely. I can't help but glance down at the T-shirt I've got on. It's pretty faded and just shows the outline of The Uglymen. Their lead singer has an afro the size of the moon – it seems to be the only thing that shows what a cool band they are. That's not the reason I chose to wear it today. It was the first thing on the floor that was clean enough for school. My gut seems to strain against the cotton. I slouch a bit to hide it.

'Hey,' says Kendo, looking around to see who he can see.

I remember something and have to speak. 'Gotta ask you about our science homework,' I say.

At the word 'homework', Kendo looks first bored then defensive. 'Me?'

'You were the only one paying attention when Mr Henderson gave us those genograms.'

'The what?'

Lewis thumps Kendo on the shoulder. 'The thing you fill in about your family.'

'Oh. What about it?'

'How do you fill it if you don't know the information?'

Kendo looks at me darkly. 'I don't give a shit about my dad.'

'I'm not talking about your dad.'

'What are you talking about?'

'I mean, if you're not sure about how to find out more information about stuff.'

'I don't know. Can't your mum tell you all you need to know?'

'I've asked her. I've still got gaps. I can't hand it in like that.' I hesitate then decide to take the plunge. 'What if there are things that Mum won't tell me?'

Lewis looks at me. 'Are you trying to find out whether there was anyone else in your family with bipolar?'

A thick silence falls. I don't think I'm the only one to notice it because Kendo sort of jerks back like he's been stung. My eyes have narrowed; I can feel them trying to stop sunlight from getting in. 'What do you mean?' I say, really slowly.

Lewis looks away, his neck flaring with red.

'Lew, what do you mean?'

He seems to make up his mind and turns his head back. He's not looking directly into my eyes, though. 'I thought you knew. Didn't you know? I mean, it'll show up if you map it on your family history.'

I stare.

'Bipolar disorder, the thing that Josh had. It's, you know, they say it's hereditary.'

If there had been quiet before, it was smothered now with the hot sound of blood in my ears. I think of Josh and his highs and lows. I think how he hated his medication and wouldn't take it. I think of the fights he had with Janet and Taylor. I think of me, being like him. I feel faint, sick, in pain. I feel lost, alone, betrayed. Finally, I suck in enough air to ask Lewis, 'How do you know? You're not a doctor.'

He shrugs but I see his answer. He isn't a doctor but he knows how to find out about diseases. He's looked it up. You were my cousin but it was Lewis who looked up your mental illness. He probably found out all about your symptoms and treatments, what would've helped and what wouldn't. He might have found out what to do when you were manic so that you wouldn't have gone up that tree like you were on fire. While I was too comatose from your death to do anything, my best friend had found the answers to the questions that I should have been asking from the moment I knew, from that first time I heard your diagnosis. And my *best friend* had not said anything to me, not a word until now. Along with my two-faced, lying, let's-keep-it-quiet-in-case-he-freaks family.

'Hey.' Lewis is trying to take a step back from his murderous words. 'It doesn't necessarily mean that anyone else in your family will get it. *You* might not get it.'

In that, I hear the words twist around until they say the thing that they really mean. You might *get it*.

When no-one says anything else for a minute, Kendo runs his hand through his hair and shrugs. 'Did you hear about Bonnie and Jordan?'

Lewis is not looking at me. 'Yeah, we know.'

'Always thought Jordan was an idiot.' Kendo sees Charlie and takes off in his direction.

Lewis looks around for a bit. I am stone next to him. He's very tall today for some reason, or maybe he's just looking up for once. He looks good. Strong. Healthy. He sees me looking. 'Sorry,' he says. 'I thought they'd told you. I thought you knew all about it. '

'I do now.'

'Don't let it…' He stops, tries again. 'Don't let it get to you.'

I shake my head, not to agree with him but to let him know that it is too late.

I get a chance to see Mr Henderson in our last period of school. We've got science and he starts the class on a revision sheet. I take the moment to go up to his desk while everyone sorts themselves.

'What can I do for you, William?'

I tuck my hands into my armpits. 'How do you know whether you're going to inherit something?'

He looks at me curiously. 'It'll be in the deceased person's will.'

My hands ball into fists and I have to put them by my side. How can teachers be so stupid sometimes?

'I mean, a disease. How can you tell whether you're going to inherit a disease?'

'Oh, sorry.' He laughs to himself. He *laughs*. I hold myself back so that I don't kill him. 'I didn't realize what you meant! You can work out the probability of inheriting conditions if you know parents' recessive or dominant genes. Genetic testing sometimes works. But most conditions are a mixture of genetic and environmental causes. It's a combination of factors that makes a condition emerge.'

'Factors?'

'Well, it's not only nature that makes things happen – nurture is involved as well.' He sees me looking blank and so tries again. 'Factors like how healthy you are. If you take drugs or not. How stable your upbringing is. What influence your friends and family have on you. Things like that.' He pauses, shuffles some papers impatiently. 'Anything else you want to know, William?'

I suddenly know too much. I shake my head and go back to my desk.

The day goes on. It doesn't even get as hot as they predicted it would so we don't even think about the pool. Lewis goes off to the library after school to get another Clive Cussler. Or maybe to avoid me. I have a work shift at 5 o'clock so I hustle Sofie home and try to eat as much as I can before I leave again. Mum walks through the door in time to see me eat the last of the spaghetti.

'That was your father's lunch for tomorrow!'

There are so many things I could say to her, so much I could fire off. I force myself to sound calm. 'Sorry, Mum,' I say, but I'm not. Oh, no, not at all. Don't leave it in the fridge if you don't want me to eat it.

She's still dark on me when I leave for Speedy Sam's Burgers. I'm wired like an electricity tower when I arrive at work. And, wouldn't you know it; the Bitch Lady is manager for the evening. I glance at the clock and think, darkly, three hours and 55 minutes to go.

It's okay for half an hour and then two busloads of hungry oldies turn up and we have to churn the burgers out thick and fast. Who said that junk food was only for the young? The people that eat the most of our stuff - except the Fat Man who lives in the flat over the (now closed) fish and chip shop - are the silver haired bus travellers who make their way through our town on the way to high adventure.

Michelle puts me on grill. That's where you load burgers onto the hot plate, turn them when the timer goes, and cook the other side. It's not hard but I'm not fast. Hey, I've only been doing this job for less than half a year and it's not like I want to get a degree in meat turning. Michelle starts up.

'Move it, princess.'

'Now, okay?'

'Jesus Christ, it'd be faster having my dog do your work.'

At least she doesn't call me Bull Burger.

At first, I ignore her. Too many other things on my mind. I concentrate on fitting the correct amount of meat on the plate and keeping the grill clean. But the oldies seem to be hungrier than ever tonight. They want two of everything, with extra cheese, extra fast.

'Come on, loser. Don't know why we even bother rostering you on.'

I work as fast as I can but the burgers are sticky and need prising apart. The others have to wait for me – you can't make up a burger without the meat. I feel them watching but I can't seem to go any faster.

'When we get a break, you're off grill,' hisses Michelle in my ear. 'You clean the freezer where it doesn't matter how slow you are.'

I look up at her, sweat dripping from my forehead and into my eyes. She has a sneer right across her face, a sort of happy-snarl of bitchiness just set for me. I see it in her eyes – she loves a victim. My hand clenches around my tongs and I go so far to lift it up an inch. She doesn't notice, though. Her thoughts are on making my life miserable. As she turns away, she's even humming. Brainchild. "Never Stay Away" (number 14).

'Cool bass line,' I say automatically. What is the matter with me?

'What?' She turns back. That must have taken effort. She usually doesn't like making any extra movement.

'The bass line in that song.' I keep talking like I'm taking myself to my own death. 'Not the hardest, but essential.'

'What would you know about it?' She takes a step towards me.

'I play it. It's not hard.'

'You play guitar?' She says it like it tastes bad.

'Yeah,' I say, more quietly. Then, 'And piano.' I suddenly want to know something about her, something that explains why she is how she is. 'Don't you play an instrument?'

The words sound wrong in the steamy kitchen, not like they'd sounded in my head, and the look on her face says it all. Contempt would be too nice a description. 'Listen, dick, some of us have to work for a living. We don't have time for school boy games.' She turns away.

The bell goes on the cooker. As I go back to it, I see the others still watching me. Someone gives a quick laugh. They have a range of expressions on their faces from amusement to sympathy. I feel my face heat up and it isn't because of the sudden blast of air from the grill. Something inside me clicks, falls and shatters.

I finish the rest of the shift in silence. No one talks to me, we're all too busy. Or maybe they choose not to. Whatever. My head is full of fuzz. Something Michelle has said hit me hard and I'm not really sure what it was. The fuzz starts to affect my arms and by the time nine o'clock comes around, I'm slow as a slug and it isn't just the cold. The freezer is fully stocked from me lugging boxes of food from the storeroom downstairs. I take off my apron, change my shirt and sling my bag over one shoulder. I leave without looking at anyone.

Dad's waiting for me in the car park. He has the window down in the car, one arm hanging out. From the door of Speedy Sam's Burgers, I can't see his face but I bet he's asleep. I walk over to him and just watch through the open window. His head is lolling back against the seat and his other hand is resting on his huge stomach. I push his shoulder. 'Dad.'

'Hey.' He comes out of sleep slowly, looking like he'd rather be there. I get in the passenger seat and slam the door. He jumps like he's forgotten me. 'Right,' he says but waits a moment before starting the car. 'Set?'

'Yeah.'

'Good shift?' He swings the car onto the road.

I shrug.

He nods back.

We travel through the quiet city. Street lights blare. A dead magpie waves a wing at us as we drive over the top of it.

'Dad?'

'Yeah?'

I take a moment to compose my question. I tell myself: calm, no rage. 'Was anyone else in our family like Uncle Len?'

Dad turns the corner, drives a while, smacks his lips together, then answers. 'What do you mean?'

'Oh, you know.' You *know*. 'You said he was wild. Strange.'

'Why do you want to know, Will?'

'I dunno.'

'Will?'

'What was wrong with him?'

Dad shrugs. 'I don't know for sure. I don't think that anyone was able to say. They reckon he was mad.'

'Mad?' I take a deep breath. 'Mad, like Josh? Did he have bipolar?'

Dad is really uncomfortable now. He wriggles in his seat and his huge hands squeeze the steering wheel. 'I don't know a lot about him, Will. He seemed okay to me. It's just that sometimes he went a bit off. I never saw him like that, though. I just know from what your Grandpa used to say.'

'You haven't answered my first question.'

He stops at the lights and drums his fingers on the steering wheel. 'What question?'

'Was anyone else mad like Great-uncle Len?'

'Mate, you're asking the wrong person. I really don't know.'

'No one on your side of the family then?'

'No.'

'What about Mum's side?'

'You'd have to ask her.'

'Would she tell me?'

He starts forward and takes so long to answer me I think he's not going to. 'Will, does it really matter?'

So maybe Dad doesn't know that I could be the same as Josh? Hasn't anyone told him either? We're pulling into our drive, over the gutter and onto the patch of weeds where Dad always parks. It seems I'm taking too long to say anything as well and Dad hauls himself out of the car without waiting for me to finish. So I think really hard before I tell myself the answer to my own question.

Yeah, it matters. It really does.

22

LEWIS

The drawings are flying out of my fingers. It's like they've been stuck inside for so long that they're stampeding their way forward. At first, there're a lot of pictures of friends at the pool lazing under that shade sail. Then they sort of zoom in on Bull who is in and out of the diving pool until he blurs.

It's funny. The more that I draw Bull, the smaller he seems to get. It starts to look so ridiculous – the enormous Bull so small against the others – that I stop. I do a quick sketch of Mum instead, soldier-like, iron-clad, talking to Dr Nightingale. Dad is in the background, the cosy chair arms wrapped around him while he tries to read the paper and ignore his Warrior Wife. I put in a beer balanced on the chair arm, cold condensed on the glass just like Dad likes it best.

Then there is another picture of Bonnie. Her hair still blocks one eye. She's waiting for Grace who arrives on the scene with that blazing look on her face that seems to strike Bull through his heart every time he sees it. I wonder if she knows how she gets to him? Grace is a gunmetal kind of girl, with ebony black eyes. Her self-inflicted tatts are a thick black as well. When I draw Grace, I can't help but press the pencil hard into the paper so that even with my eyes closed I can trace her shape. I like drawing Grace because she's so clear but she spoils the tips of the lead and makes the back of the paper unusable so I don't draw her much. People like Grace, you have to protect yourself against them.

I try to put Bull on the page with the girls but he's avoiding Bonnie and not ready for Grace and is stubbornly refusing to get any bigger. Come on Bull, I think. You have to get your act together. It's going to be alright, you just got to believe it.

It's hard to think about Bull when I'm feeling so good. When I first met Bull I knew I was seeing a fellow sufferer. And I know I said something today that cut him real bad. I'm sorry about that, really, but just at the moment, right now and right here, I need to concentrate on the *wellness* of everyone I know. I need Mum's strength and Bonnie's independence and even the day-to-day casualness of Charlie and Kendo who go about their lives as if it's all a bit of a practice for the real thing. I'm sick of sickness. I want to get off that boat for good.

23

BULL

Our sometimes-band is playing in the music room.
'*Love me, hold me…*'
This song is definitely not, and never will be, on my list.

Morgan's trying to eat a peanut butter sandwich in between singing bits of *Rollercoaster,* a new song that someone – probably Mitch – thought would be good for us. The peanut butter turns the words into: '*Nuvme, holme…*'

It's not working and it's not all Morgan and his sandwich's fault. The bass line is a dull thud thud while Mitch's guitar carries the whole song. That's the problem. It's his song and that's why he chose it. The rest of us are just going along for the ride.

Tash slams down her sticks. 'This is crap. Morgan, stuff that bread in your mouth and swallow. We can't do anything until you finish.'

My stomach growls. I've left my lunch in my bag and I'm staring too hard at Morgan's crusts as he jams them down his throat. I strum to myself. Mitch answers with a crazy section of bars he just does every now and then.

'Okay,' says Morgan. 'Ready.'

'About time.' Tash poises. 'From the start. One, two.'

We start off alright this time, Morgan only coughing once as breadcrumbs stick in his neck. He gets through two versus and two choruses, and I'm wincing at the bad lyrics, before Mitch takes over for a full minute while the song soars. I plod along with my four chord changes, dulled into submission. Morgan finishes with another chorus. We stop and look at him.

'Well,' he says. 'Okay.'

Tash sighs.

Mitch does his own section again.

'Stop that,' I say louder than I need to. I slam my mouth shut.

'What's wrong with you?' Mitch says, still playing, softer though.

I shrug, feeling dark.

'That was alright,' Morgan offers. 'Want to do it again?'

'What else have we got?' Tash says, her arms crossed.

'What else do you want to do?'

'Something that has better words.'

Morgan sings, '*Love me, hold me, on our rollercoaster ride.*'

'Crap,' says Tash.

'You choose,' says Morgan to his sister.

Tash does her drum solo, smashing the skins and cymbals. We've all got the bits we do well by ourselves but we don't play well together. I pull the strap off my shoulder and put my bass into its bag.

'We finished?' says Mitch, surprised. He's still playing, so softly I can hardly hear but I know he's doing it. I want to rip his guitar out of his hands and smash it on the amp. Instead, I zip my bag closed. The noise rips through the air.

'Looks like it,' says Morgan.

'You keep going,' I say. 'I've gotta be somewhere.' I grab my guitar by the neck.

'Where?' I hear Morgan but I'm already out the door.

I don't have to be anywhere. I particularly don't have to be here, in this music room, with this bunch of wannabees. I go to the storeroom, stow my bass away, and stare for a minute at the costume rack. Somehow, it doesn't tempt me. Its shadows don't seem dark enough or maybe the shadows in me seem blacker than anything living. I go out into the sun and get stabbed by the searing heat. The shadows don't budge, though.

'Hey, Bull.' Lewis is sitting on the ground under the eave. He has his earphones in, knees pulled up, forearms casually on them, fingers tapping to his music (my number 100). I slide down next to him but not too close. I hear his words in my ears like he's just said them: *you might not get it.* My hands are clenched.

We stare into the empty yard in front of us. Even on the dusty shady ground, the heat swirls around us and makes me sweat. I wonder whether Lewis is hiding out here but he's still beating to the music, his face relaxed. He's been a different guy this week, not quite in the here-and-now but happy. Didn't he notice what his words did to me? Didn't he guess how much he spun me out? I thought I could count on him to help me but it seems like he's not here for me at the moment. He's too *well.*

'You're good,' I say accidentally.

'What?' Lewis pulls an ear bud out and turns to me.

'I said, you're good. You're well. This week. Better than you have been.'

He nods. 'BGL 5.1 this morning.' He grins and puts his thumb up so I figure that must be the equivalent of getting A on the diabetes exam.

'Great,' I say. 'Terrific.' And I am glad for him. But what about me?

He puts his music back in, nodding at me or nodding to the beat, I'm not sure. I look at him sideways so that he doesn't notice. I can't believe that long lanky body of his crawls with disease. It doesn't seem right.

Then suddenly I'm thinking of you and what crept into your body, poisoning your mind as it went. How did that feel? Was it like when Lewis got a hypo and sank into a sort of babbling mess like he did at that all-nighter at Kendo's over the holidays? Did you feel your sickness in your pores, in your bones, or did it just tear at your head, turning your grey matter blue? Was it gradual or did it attack you like a tiger in the night? What's it going to feel like when it happens to *me*?

'You right, Bull?' Lewis has his eyes on me. They're very clear and see right inside me. 'You're sweating heaps.'

I wipe the stream from my forehead. 'Hot out here.' My heart's racing again.

'Let's go,' he says, unfurling his legs to stand up. 'I need a drink. You got any money?'

I stumble up. The heat seems to be wrapped around my legs, holding me down. I fight against it and sweat even more. Lewis is staring at me. I fumble around in my pocket, pull out a few gold coins.

'Sweet,' Lewis says.

He leads the way inside to our standard vending machine that's outside the double classroom. This time it's me who has the sickly sports drink while he sculls cold water. I feel the sugar rush do its trick and get a glimpse, I think, of what it feels like to be Lewis sometimes. Some of my energy returns and the sweat slows.

We perch on a table, not really allowed inside but it's where everyone is hiding from the heat. The lack of movement in the room is unreal, a sort of testament to how hot everyone is. Girls sit with their dresses pulled up as high as they can, guys flap their sticky shirts away from their sweaty chests. For once, no one gives a shit about the rules or even about how they look. I see Morgan and Mitch lounging in the corner. Their heads are down as they talk.

'Storm coming,' says Lewis and I look out the window to where he's pointing. Black clouds are gathering on the edge of the sky. I can't wait until they get to the sun.

It takes the rest of the school day, though. The bell rings and Lewis goes off to his classes and me to mine. By the time everything's finished and I get to Sofie's school, the sky is furious. The sun is smothered but the heat is trapped, leaving me feeling wound up and still as hot as I was.

Sofie walks slowly to the gate, her hair ratty from a day running around. She doesn't even say hello when she sees me but gives a small puckering of her mouth in recognition. We walk home without saying anything. Occasionally, her shoulder brushes my arm as if making sure I'm still there. It's annoying and feels like small electric shocks.

Mum is home. She's in her oldest bag dress, the orange one that sticks to her in the wrong places and she only puts on when the temperature is max. 'What are you doing here?' says Sofie, sounding tired.

'The air-conditioner broke down at work. They had to send us home.'

I put my bag on the floor and go for the fridge.

'In your room, William.'

'What?' I say, my head buried in the frosty coolness.

'Your bag lives in your room.'

There's something odd in her voice that makes me pull out of the fridge and look at her. Despite the old dress and the fact that she's not at work, she looks boiling hot. Her face is red and blotchy, like she's been jogging. She's standing, hands on hips, staring at me. 'I'm just getting a drink, Mum.'

'And you can't put your bag in your room first?' She gives it a poke with her foot. 'I've just cleaned up.'

I shut the fridge door and look around the kitchen. It is just the same as it always is. No dirty plates in sight. No bread on the bench. No jars of honey, Vegemite or jam. Seven oranges are arranged on a bowl in a pattern that would be completely ruined if you ate one. The floor shines. My bag is a black blob on the lino. I feel my head tighten into a headache. 'I just wanted a drink.'

'You're not dying of thirst, William. You could wait the ten seconds it took you to put your bag where it should be.'

It must be the heat. Let it be the heat. I pick up my bag, walk around Mum who is still standing with those rigid arms, and go through the lounge with its fat cushions in rows on the couch and the lamp in the exact middle of the top of the piano to my room. I throw my bag in a corner, turn the fan on high and fling myself on the bed face down. I see the genogram sticking out from under the bed where I shoved it once Mr Henderson had given me a C, and push it further under, feeling sick.

At least my room is comfortably *untidy*. No point in putting things away when you're going to need them sooner or later. Mum doesn't touch my room. Or the girls' rooms. But the rest of the house is like a hospital – hygienic and dust free even though it's an old shambly place. It strikes me that it's so clean it's weird. It's even a bit crazy, if you think about it.

I stay here for a while but I really am dying of thirst, no matter what Mum says. I strip off my school clothes, pull on a pair of shorts and go out into the kitchen. Mum's gone, hopefully to have a refreshing long cold shower, and so I pull out stuff for a snack. My headache has worsened but I'm starving. I make peanut butter sandwiches – Morgan's have been bugging me all day – and an iced chocolate, and take them to the lounge to splodge. I've only taken one bite before there's a screech from the kitchen.

Mum.

Not refreshed, obviously. Worse than ever, obviously.

'What do I have to do to be heard around here?'

I'm sort of listening but don't really think the words are for me. Suddenly she's there at the couch, leaning over the back of it, hands grasping the top. 'What?' I say, loudly.

'Didn't you just hear me? I've just *cleaned up*.' She's almost spitting with rage.

'I know, you keep telling me.' She's too close, too close.

'Then you *are* hearing me but you're just *ignoring* me.'

I stand up to get away from her, the sandwich sour in my mouth. 'Mum, what are you talking about?'

She doesn't say anything but points with one very long, very ugly finger. 'Your mess in the kitchen!'

I look past her to the kitchen bench. I can just see the peanut butter jar, open. Bread slices have flopped out of their bag. 'I'll clean it up in a minute.'

'You'll clean it up now!'

Her face is furious. Red has now gone to beetroot. My own face is hot, though. I'm bubbling lava. 'Mum, what is *wrong* with you? I'm just eating a sandwich and then I'll go and clean it up. That should be okay.'

'*Should* be okay? No, William, it is *not* okay. I work all day and expect to come home to a place that has been kept relatively clean while I was away particularly when I've just spent hours cleaning it up!'

'You haven't been at work all day. You're home now.'

She snaps. I see it as a flush of something smacked across her face. '*You will clean it up now!*'

But I'm my mother's son. 'No. I won't. I'll do it later.' I take a bite out of my sandwich.

She's so quick I don't see it coming but the rest of my bread flies out of my hand as she slaps it away. It lands, peanut butter side down, on Dad's lounge chair.

We stare at it. I'm the first to turn away. I look at my mother. Her shoulders are heaving. The orange dress has slipped and it's skewwhiff around her middle. 'You are weird,' I say to her slowly. 'There is something *definitely* wrong with you.'

She gapes at me. Her hand goes to her throat. I don't care.

Yeah, I go and clean the kitchen. I put the bread and the peanut butter and the margarine in the bin. I pull the bag out and tie its top. Then I take it outside to the garbage. She's still in the lounge room but on her knees in front of Dad's chair, dabbing at the brown fatty mess of peanut butter and bread. I leave her to it and walk away.

24

LEWIS

Bonnie fainted in the heat during the last class of school. Grace gave a grunt and was suddenly on the floor next to her friend. Ms O'Grady, the art teacher, swished over in her layers of purple silk and bent down over Bonnie. The two of them rolled her over into the coma position but Bonnie woke up. Her dress had ridden up so that the edge of her blue underpants could be seen. She seemed to know that straight away and tugged at her uniform as the first thing she did. She was pale like a vampire. The teacher made her lie still and I watched as the colour seeped back into her cheeks.

The page in front of me has one single person on it. The colour – rose madder lake that I smudge lightly – is coming back into her cheeks. Her black hair flares out behind her leaving her face free. Her position is that, depending on how you look at the page, she could be lying on her side or she could be running. I give her jeans to wear, runners on her feet, although the line of blue that edged her in real life has burnt into my eyes. I draw her an azure singlet, firm across her chest, and feel light-headed when I do. Azure becomes my favourite colour.

The pages of this new non-Keally notebook are filling fast. When I count back, I've got more pictures of Bonnie than of anyone else. I shut the book carefully.

'Lewis,' calls Mum. 'Dinner.'

The Judge likes dinner on time. She *can* vary but she doesn't like it and she especially doesn't like it when Dad or I don't get there quick enough after she calls. Sometimes Dad misses dinner but she doesn't wait.

Tonight, the smell of sausages drifts through the house. I park myself in front of a plate filled with three of them. 'Lamb and rosemary,' says Mum, looking satisfied.

'Can't we have plain ones for once?' grumbles the old man but is silenced by a glare. I hide a grin.

'How was school?' Mum asks.

I nod, mouth full. She takes that as a 'fine.'

'How was work?'

This time, it's Dad who has a full mouth and can only grunt. Well, it might be that his mouth is full and the grunt is a result of this but I find it hard sometimes to tell the difference between Dad having a full mouth and his normal speech.

The storm crashes overhead and the power goes off. We can't see our sausages to eat.

'Goddamnuselesselectricity,' mutters Mum.

We sit in the charcoal darkness and watch each other when the flashes of lightning give us fleshy tones. Dad has his eyes closed. Mum has her face in her hands. Dad, I think, is waiting this out like he does with everything. Mum is angry because she can't control the storm. I wonder how my parents ever got together and whether they regret it.

Me? I wait the storm out as well because there's nothing you can really do about it. The light flickers back on after about ten minutes and my snags are cold and greasy. We start eating again like nothing has happened. Except for Mum. She finishes quickly and takes her plate away. I look at Dad but he's got his eyes closed again. For a second, meat catches in my throat. He opens his eyes, looks at me in a direct, heavy stare before slogging away at his dinner.

Thunder rolls, a slow deep moan of something about to happen.

25

BULL

Y*ou will clean it up now!*
No.

No, no. no.

There is something definitely *wrong with you.*

Words spin in my head. Number 44, loud and angry and red, slams around in there as well.

I walk a long way before the rain starts, great fat summer drops. I forgot I knew that a storm was coming. I think that the darkness is me, that the clouds are inside me not outside. I only have shorts on. I am drenched in seconds.

Summer rain is fierce but not cold. I walk on through it, barefoot. The footpath is warm from the day's heat. Steam tries to rise but is beaten by the torrent of water. The further I walk, the more the gutters fill until I have a creek running beside me that pulls dirt and sticks and leaves with it. And me. I follow the water until it is unexpectedly sucked into a drain, disappearing at speed underground. Rain runs off me almost as fast. I stare into the water wondering what it would be like to be taken down into the darkness.

A car horn toots. I look up to see a strange blue sedan trying to pull up on the kerb without getting swamped by the water. A figure through the steamed up window is waving at me but I've got no idea who it is. I'm so wet – do they really want me to get in? But the door of the car opens and now it seems I've got no choice but to wade through the swamp to get to the car. I try to wipe as much rain off as I can but there's no point. I slide into the back seat, bringing the weather with me.

'Use this.'

A towel lands on my head and I rub myself over as quickly as I can, glancing up to see a woman driver watching the road and not me. Bonnie's in the passenger's seat. I keep drying myself, more slowly now, feeling the icy blast of the car's air-conditioner on my wet skin and suddenly conscious that I've only got shorts on and I'm a big, half-naked guy in the back of a car with two females. I move further into the corner of the seat. 'Thanks,' I say, not sure that I mean it.

'You got caught out,' says the woman matter-of-factly and I nod.

'Are you alright?' Bonnie turns in her seat. I notice that her hair is wet as well.

'You got caught, too?' I say because I'm not alright. Not trapped in her car, not anywhere near this close to her.

'Only a little bit. Mum was picking me up at school.'

'I was late.' Bonnie's mum doesn't sound apologetic. Bonnie shrugs.

We're going past the petrol station. 'You can drop me off here if you want,' I say. 'I'll ring Dad. He can pick me up.'

'Might as well take you home.' Bonnie's mum doesn't even slow down.

'Thanks.'

I lean back, trying not to get the seat too wet. I wedge the towel under my bum to sop up the water from my shorts. I've got goose bumps from the aircon. I fold my arms across my chest. Bonnie notices and fiddles with the control. The ice blast stops and the car begins to humidify again.

Bonnie's school bag is beside me. We all have the same standard issue black bag but the girls put ribbons and key rings on theirs to tell them apart. Bonnie has three ribbons, all shades of pink. I know my bag because of the big rip across the outside pocket. You did that with the pocket knife Taylor got you for your sixteenth birthday. I feel my heart rate quicken. I was trying hard not to think of you while I was in Bonnie's car but it's too late. In faint letters on Bonnie's bag, coloured over with black Texta that looks pearly green on the webbed fabric, I see *Bonnie heart Josh*. I give the bag a shove with my leg and the letters move out of sight.

The car slows. We're at my place. I look up to see Bonnie's mum watching me in the rear vision mirror. I realize that I hadn't given her any directions and neither had Bonnie. She just knew where I lived. I expect kids at school to know but not parents. Was I poor Josh's cousin that didn't cope very well when you died? Does the whole town know where I live? Did they make a special point of walking past, going 'That's where he lives. You know, that kid that's seeing a shrink because his cousin fell out of a tree'?

I open the door without waiting for the car to stop completely, scooping the towel up as I go. 'Thanks,' I say again and slam the door closed. The rain continues. I'm wet again as bad as before within seconds. I cross over the mud and crap that's our nature strip and run around the back without looking at the car. I can't really hear whether it has driven off because of the noise of the rain but I reckon that once I'm out of sight it'll go. I put the towel around my shoulders and sit on the back step, shivering slightly. Our back yard is a disgusting mess of summer-dry ground that's underwater. I close my eyes and wait for the storm to stop.

THE WEATHER IS A TALKING point at school. The rain was too much and too sudden, and houses were flooded. Everyone's scared that our town will be like last year's Lockyer Valley. Kendo says his garage was underwater and that his Mum's car filled up. Hard to believe when I saw his mum bring him to school this morning. Charlie's sister's guinea pig drowned. The girls cry at that and a couple even give him a hug. How's that fair? It wasn't even his pet.

I see Bonnie across the room sitting with a heavily eye-lined Grace. Mum washed and dried the towel, and it's in my bag to give back to her. I will. Later. Mrs McWilliams comes in and starts to hand out a history pop test. Brilliant. A great start to the day.

'A quick test of what we've covered so far this term,' she says without a trace of humour. I glance through the questions. Most of them are, of course, dates. When other teachers give out quizzes, they try to liven them up with stupid answers to questions like 'Who wrote Macbeth? A) Hamlet B) J.K. Rowling C) The Bard D) Banquo.' Not Mrs Mac. Every one of her questions is potentially deadly if answered wrong. I will be dead twenty times over with this.

Then she says, 'I hope you are remembering to record

your own histories in your notebooks' and a light flashes in my brain. I seem to zoom out of my body for a moment, so while the class is groaning and muttering and chewing their pens I get this sudden look at me sitting white-faced next to Lewis. History. That's where I've seen your notebook before. It was your history assignment.

Your last history assignment. Your last bit of history. You are history now.

I don't like the way that sometimes when I think of you I seem to fold in on myself. It's like I constantly get bombarded with thoughts that I can't control. Mr Petersen says it will get easier in time. The Bereavement Centre said that grief travels its own course and everything I'm feeling is normal. But, Josh, sometimes I just can't get you out of my mind. You are a parasite in my head.

Lewis elbows me in the ribs. 'Bull,' he says, 'wake up.'

I come crashing down into my seat again and turn towards him. It feels like a big effort.

'Come on,' he says. 'Get with it.'

He says that like he hadn't noticed my pain but this is *Lewis* here. He understands. Yes? This time he doesn't want to look at me, he's got his pen circling answers – any answers – to the quiz, but I know that he knows I'm spaced. He wouldn't usually *say* anything to me but he'd *look* like he understood and that would be enough to let me know that I'm not alone. Not today. I elbow him back but he won't look up. He doesn't want to know me at the moment. It's because he's well and I'm…well, I don't know what I am.

I put my head down and circle all the 'A's. I'm doing the shivering thing again. It seems to come on a lot lately. The words in front of me are in another language. I'm thinking about what I can remember from your notebook. That crazy writing and those black pages showing the climb and fall moments of your year. And the picture of Great Uncle Len. *Our* Great Uncle Len. It strikes me that your history is my history as well.

Mrs Mac reads the answers out and Lewis grabs my page to correct it, shoving his in front of me. I tick all his answers and write *20/20 Excellent Work Lewis* on the bottom of his page. He gives me a zero.

Gradually, the monotony of class soothes me. By the end, you let go your grip and I'm a bit more with it. I can go out with the others and eat biscuits and laugh at more of Kendo's flood stories – by now, paint tins were floating in the garage water and his brother's old kayak came off its hooks – and even add one of my own. 'I went swimming in the rain,' I say. 'Nothing but my boardies on.'

'And we picked you up.' Bonnie's voice is high above the others. Kendo hoots and grins slyly. 'Bonnie picked you up?'

Now they're all laughing except for me. And Bonnie. Her face is dark and her hair flops over her eye. Lewis isn't laughing either. He's got *his* eyes on Bon and I see his hand clench and unclench. 'Well,' I say, 'I'm a good looking guy. Especially just in my shorts.'

That makes Lewis look at me and there's a hint of laughter in his eyes. Thanks, mate, I think, but not sarcastically. Lew and me, we know the facts. We aren't tanked like Kendo and we aren't like Charlie who looks like he's done growing. We aren't finished yet, we aren't man-shaped, and sometimes that isn't good but it's a fact.

I catch Grace's eyes. She's standing next to Bonnie who has turned away in disgust. Grace isn't laughing. She's looking in that hard way she has – like she's looking down a microscope – but staring maybe a bit longer than she needs to. Did I imagine that? I mean, why would she do that? Because I'm some sort of ugly slug? Because she –

dare I even think it – likes me? I raise my eyebrows. Her face softens as her lips curl up in an almost undetectable smile.

The bell goes. That's it. We break up, move onto the next thing. Kendo slings his drink into the bin and of course it sprays Coke everywhere. Girls squeal. Boys laugh. I think about how easy it is for things to happen and then disappear from everyone else's mind except mine.

Lewis has geography. I've got sport. We're going our separate ways. 'Got anything on after school?' he says.

'Nuh.'

'Wanna go to the pool?'

I look out at the still-stormy sky. 'And get electrocuted?'

Lewis shrugs.

'I've got to get Sofie first.'

Lewis looks at me, weighs things up, and gives me another chance. From what, I'm not sure. 'I'll come with you.'

'Meet you at the gate.'

He's restless, I think. He feels good but it feels wrong to him. Usually, he has to go straight home after school to eat etc. But I'm glad he didn't want to, glad of the company, really. Glad of the chance to keep you out of my thoughts.

26

LEWIS

I wait for Bull after school, rocking on my feet. He takes a long time. Finally, we walk together to get Sofie, talking shit all the way.

'Couldn't go out with Jules.'

'Nah. Too girly.'

'Could go out with Mina.'

Mina's in Year Eleven.

'Like she'd go out with you.'

'Mina or Bethany. Both hot.'

I push Bull, even though I don't have a chance of moving his bulk. I do it all the same. Bull shoves me and my body whips back like a sapling and snaps upright again. We look at each other and then away because we know we've just had about the emptiest conversation we've ever had in our lives. Is there something wrong?

Sofie is waiting at her primary school, sitting on the gate.

'You're late.'

She looks angry to me but I don't really know how a

little sister acts. Maybe this is normal? 'My fault,' I say quickly. 'Blame me.'

She doesn't seem to care but jumps down from the gate and walks away in front of us. I raise an eyebrow at Bull who shrugs. Must be normal.

We walk in silence and I get a chance to think about normal. This must be it, walking to get your little sister. Having responsibility other than yourself. That makes sense. I nod to myself.

'You okay?' says Bull.

'Great, mate.' I grin. 'I'm fantastic.'

And I am, too. Utterly normal, completely bloody fantastic.

We get rid of Sofie at Bull's house where Ella is just home from training and keep walking to the pool. The sky is dark and dangerous – dark violet on storm grey - but the action is a long distance away. Lightning flashes but we can't hear any thunder. We swim for a while, mucking around in the deep end with the others, then eat junk from the pool canteen. Hot chips and lolly pythons never tasted so good. Charlie and Kendo, Jules and three girls I don't know enough to remember their names, join us. Bonnie is nowhere to be seen and I don't feel like checking anyone else out, despite what I said to Bull. Grace isn't here either. Bull doesn't even glance at the other girls. I think about the stupid things we said after school and cringe. Since when did Bull and I become bullshit artists? Maybe when we're in a pack but never when it's just the two of us. It makes me feel strange, like there's something there that wasn't before.

I watch the clouds begin their move on us. They're like blunt-headed sharks swimming across the sky. They creep up on the sun and make it send out tendrils of light in distress that spear the darkening water of the pool. I get a thrill of fear in my stomach for no real reason at all and have to look around at the talking, joking, dripping group of friends in front of me to make it stop. And there's Bull, lying face down on his towel, unreadable. No help at all.

27

BULL

When I get home from the pool, I go straight to the piano and tackle Opus 10.

Ella is in her usual telly-watching position. 'Will! Be quiet. I'm watching *Friends*!'

Fifth bar, sixth, seventh.

'Will! Shut up! Shut up, shut up, shut up!'

11th bar, 12th, 13th.

From the corner of my eye I see Ella sulking into the couch, arms folded and knees pulled up to her chest.

18th, 19th. I stretch it further. If I tune out the rest of the world, I can see the shape of the piece in front of me. I know it in my head, have listened to it one million times. I stare so hard at the music in front of me that the room goes blurry around the edges and I can pretend that I'm Chopin, sitting in my drawing room, making music.

Well, not really. Chopin was a genius and I am definitely not.

I read a newspaper article ages ago that said geniuses are made, not born, and that it's all about how much effort you make. You have to work five times harder than the average person, and keep going for ten years. You need so much fire in your belly that it resembles a volcano. In the article, experts said that if you spend 10,000 hours concentrating on one activity you'll get to genius level. So if you spend 10,000 hours practicing handballs or drop kicks or hoop shots, then you'll be a brilliant sports star. Or 10,000 hours at the piano and you'll be a concert pianist. You also need people to support you and teach you and tell you when you're good and when you're bad. The reason Chopin was so good at what he did was that he spent a hell of a long time doing it and the people around him let him. So if I play the piano for 10,000 hours, and get Dad to tell me I'm a musical genius, then I'll be as good a musician as Chopin.

That's when this expert theory breaks down. I know I'll never be a Chopin or a Sting or even a Simon Chapman who used to go to school with us and now plays for the State Chamber Orchestra. No matter how much I love this – and I do, I love this music thing - I could practise for ten years but I don't think I'd ever get there. It's not in me to be a genius in music or anything else. Genius is inherited, it's just gotta be. It's somewhere in your genes, hidden in the code, waiting to emerge if you give it the chance. Waiting like a disease. Genius is a type of disease but one that everyone wants. Not like other things that might be lurking around waiting for their chance to take you over.

I don't have the genius disease but what about…

Mum comes in the back door, slamming her keys down on the bench so that they ring in their usual way.

'Mum!' yells Ella without taking her eyes from the telly. 'Tell Will to stop playing the piano while I'm watching TV.'

Time seems to freeze. I stop what I'm doing but don't lift my fingers from the keys. The piano sings to a sigh and then is quiet. Ella has shrunk into the cushions again but this time she's trying to hide. We wait, breath held, for Mum to explode like Mt Vesuvius.

'Will, don't play the piano while your sister is watching important television.'

It's Dad, not Mum. He's had her car while he took it to be serviced. Her keys but him driving. Ella laughs, relieved. 'See, Will?'

Dad comes and leans over the back of the couch. 'Let him play, girlie,' he says, tickling Ella. 'I think it's probably more important than what you're watching.'

I win. I grin at El and Dad looks up at me. He's smiling, still tickling Ella who squirms hard but doesn't really try to get away. 'Dad, stop,' she says, giggling. 'We thought you were Mum.'

He stops and stands up straight, rubbing his hands on his stomach. 'Yeah, I look like her, don't I? And I sound like her, too.'

'You don't yell like her.' The words are out of my mouth before I can stop them.

Dad goes sad. His body sags a bit and his face drops. It would be funny if it wasn't so real. 'You just need to give her some space, William. She's had a few things on her plate, Janet moving and all that.'

I turn back to the étude and try again. For some reason, I run through it without too many problems, to bar twenty-two anyhow. I turn to Dad but it looks like he hasn't heard a note I've played. 'Do you understand, Will?' he says.

'What?'

'Give Mum some space.'

He's serious! I could tell him a thing or two about space and Mum but I do a bit of a nod to say I'm listening. I've been giving Mum and me as much space as I can manage and I'm not going to stop now. In the back of my head, I know that's not exactly what he's suggesting but I block it out. I run through my twenty-two bars three times in a row, getting faster. Allegro, allegro.

'Will.' It's Dad, a little louder than normal. 'It could be time to stop now.'

Dad is in his armchair, pushed back into recliner position. The news is on the telly. Ella is still on the couch, looking at me. She thinks she's won. I keep my eyes on her and play the first two bars over and over. She scowls.

'William.' Dad is getting angry. The news reports more deaths on the highway.

I turn back to the piano but don't play. Chopin's drawing room has well and truly disappeared. I feel cheated. Imagine if Chopin had been born into this family? And what if he had gone to an ordinary school where most of the kids thought that football ruled and music sucked?

So Chopin didn't like football and wanted to play the piano all the time. But he didn't have all the time. He spent five hours a day at school and then some more working for a greasy hamburger place to get some cash. When he came home, he played for ten minutes and then was told by his family that they couldn't hear the television. This Chopin played every chance he could and did some composing but it wasn't really like the stuff that Pinpricks or The Uglymen played and so he didn't perform it because no one at school understood. And he couldn't get an orchestra together except for the one at his school and the kids in that wanted to play pirate songs and not the stuff that he had written.

It was just too hard. Chopin stopped playing except for the weekends when the rest of his family went out. Then he played so hard his fingers ached and his head boomed and when the rest of the family came home they yelled at him because he hadn't got the washing in and now it was wet or he hadn't walked the dog and it was getting fat or he hadn't mowed the weeds and the house looked neglected.

He took up football and broke three fingers in his first home match and sat on the bench for the rest of the season. That's when he wrote "…inside something gnaws at me…" but no one ever read it because when he died he was just like the rest of us and no one outside his family really cared. He was only remembered while someone kept his photo.

A bit like Great Uncle Len.

I look over at the sideboard, checking the photos that have stood there as long as I can remember. There aren't any of you. You were meant to still be here, Josh. You weren't meant to join Grandpa on the sideboard.

What if Chopin had a cousin like you, Josh? A friend that disappeared on him. Just like that. What would have happened to his music then?

I stand up and leave the piano. Dad gives me a look but really he's focused on the news. El has her head down over her music player. I go to my room and sit on the bed with my arms wrapped around my stomach. Even with my eyes shut, I see my room and all its things. I see Len's photo in the bookshelf and your notebook tucked beside my bed and my guitar and my shit everywhere. I feel numb but angry, empty but exploding. I wish we hadn't been cousins, I wish I'd never known you.

Why does this happen? I think of you, and then I can't stop thinking of you. It's like pulling the stitches from a cut that hasn't healed. It's like knocking myself on the head with a stone until I'm bleeding. Can't I just leave it alone? Leave *you* alone?

I go under my doona, into the smothering darkness,

and plug my ear buds in to listen to my top 20. If I shut my eyes, sometimes I can imagine that I'm in a studio somewhere where the band plays with their headphones on and sing to each through their microphones. I do it now, think about me in the background, standing behind vocals, adding the rhythm, holding it all together for the others. That's what a bass player does: gives support.

I must have fallen asleep like that because I wake up sweating with the music still going. I crawl out and breathe in some fresh air. My head clears a bit. Your notebook – your history, my history – has slipped out and weighs on my leg. I kick it off onto the floor but I can still feel the pressure of it on my skin. I push the doona right off the bed and sit cross legged on the sheet. Now I'm shivering because of the cooling sweat on my skin.

In the middle of the night like this, bad thoughts fly like demons into my head. I lean over and grab my phone and text Lewis. *Wot u doin?* I hold the phone in my hand and wait for an answer. He doesn't give me one so I figure either his battery is flat or he's turned it off or he's sleeping like a dog. I turn the phone over and over. I just wanted to ask him if he knew he was going to get sick. If there were any signs or a gut feeling of some sort that things were wrong. Because I want to know how to read the signs or any gut feelings I might get. I want to know whether I'm getting sick as well.

———

IN THE MORNING, the sun glares into my room and wakes me by smacking a ray into my head. I feel like shit from not enough sleep. Dreams, too. Not the nightmares but a whole series of dreams that whirled through my brain in a haze of smoky black. Too many to make sense of them. I check my phone. Lewis hasn't answered.

Nothing for it but to stagger out into the kitchen. Mum is there, apron on, cutting sandwiches for Dad. She takes the crusts off and lays them neatly in a row on the bench. I'm not sure why she does that – the cutting of the crusts, I mean. I wonder if the guys at Dad's work laugh at his crustless sandwiches. I'm not sure why she has to line the crusts up either. As I reach for the kettle, I make sure my arm brushes against them so that they move out of formation. Mum doesn't shift them back and I feel relieved at that even though she looks at me darkly.

We haven't had much to say to each other since the Day of the Peanut Butter Sandwich. Mum's been busy at work which means she doesn't come home until nearly tea time. Even though we help, it's still a crazy time of night especially when Sofie needs to tell Mum all about her day and then have her reading listened to and her book signed. I usually go to my room after dinner. That's my place. I strum or do homework or listen to Pinpricks. I reckon that I normally spend about one hour a day in Mum's company. Lately, it's been less.

I eat breakfast perched at the end of the bench. Another hot day's coming. I feel it creep into the house. The radio news tells more dismal tales of car accidents and terrorist bombings. I wish I'd skipped brekky. As it is, I leave half a slice of toast, slipping it into the bin when Mum's not looking.

In my room, I text Lewis again. He answers, *c u @ skool.*

School is a wash of bad odours and it's not even nine o'clock. Too many kids riding in on a non-airconditioned bus or pushing up the hill on their bikes. Ella veers off to her locker. I go to English, slipping the bag from my wet shoulder and plucking my shirt away from my skin.

'Hot, isn't it?'

Grace is the only other one in the class. She sits looking tired. She sits looking beautiful. 'Yeah,' I say idiotically. 'Hot.'

'How's Chopin?'

'What?' Then I remember our music store episode. I think of what Chopin wrote. 'Tortured,' I say.

'Really?' Grace leans forward so that her elbow is on the desk. I see the back of her hand is covered in a swirling black pattern. 'I thought he was one of the un-tortured ones.'

'*Inside something gnaws at me*,' I quote in a voice that's suddenly deep and quiet. '*Desire for life, and in the next instant, desire for death.*' It's spooky but I've remembered this bit by heart. Is it a sign?

I look at Grace but she's not acting like I'm mad. She has me caught in that look, the one that makes me think she's probing my soul. I am a hooked fish and don't even struggle. Grace frowns, not at me but at something inside her head. 'They were all tortured. Maybe the music did it to them.'

I have a vision of Chopin full of different desires crouched over his piano, concentration blocking out the rest of the world. I hear Grace's words slowly as they sink beneath my skin. 'What do you mean?'

'Those composers. So many of them were mad.' She shifts her weight to her other arm. The black pattern on this hand is detailed, complicated, frightening. 'I think the music *made* them mad.'

I shake my head. 'No. It was the time when they lived. Things were different back then.'

Grace shakes her head. She seems so certain about this

I am confused. 'It's no different to now. Look at Kurt Cobain. Tortured. Don't you think it's possible that he was driven mad by the music?'

I have never ever thought of this. Why *hadn't* I thought of this? I rub my sweating palms on my legs trying to think of something that would make Grace wrong. 'Not all musical geniuses are mad.'

'No. Not all.' Grace twirls a strand of hair around her silver-ringed finger. 'You've just got to think, though. For some people, there might be a link.'

My head is whirling again but not with night dreams. I'm thinking about how my life would be without music in it. Then I think about how my life would be if I were mad. I think, of course, about you. I think about that bad family gene and wonder what set it off in your case. You weren't the least bit musical, despite the guitar episode. It was not music that caused what you had.

The rest of the class moves in and I lose sight of Grace as others crowd around and I turn to the front of the class. It's too hot to concentrate. I'm too *disturbed* to concentrate. Every word Mr Lancefield says seems to be interfering with my head and not letting me think my thoughts through. I finish English in a state of absolute confusion. So much so that I don't notice Lewis in front of me until he punches me in the arm. But it doesn't hurt. Not straight away. Then it does. I yelp. Then the pain seeps through and I see Lewis, tall and skinny, in front of me.

28

LEWIS

Bull is sitting like a blob, pale, with his mouth open and a blank look on his face. I punch him to make him react.

He yells in shock. 'Hey!'

'We need to talk.'

I drag him away until we're outside in the roaring sun that everyone else is avoiding. He doesn't notice the toxic orpiment light.

'What's up?' he says slowly, squinting into my face.

At this point, I still want to help him but I feel angry at the way he's just standing there looking dumb. 'You. *You're* up. You're slipping, mate.'

He just stands there.

'You're going backwards. You have to catch yourself. You have to stop.'

He blinks. 'What are you going on about?'

I try again. 'You were getting better. These last few weeks, though, you're getting worse. Like before. Sick, like before. You have to stop it.'

He watches me talking then shakes his head. 'I'm not the sick one. You are.'

I laugh at that. I'm so well that I'm trying to help him! Doesn't he get it? 'I'm not sick.'

He shakes his head again. Anger sparks his eyes. 'You're not making sense. You have diabetes. You're the sick one.' He pokes his finger into my stomach.

He couldn't be any more wrong. 'I am not sick!'

He smiles at me like I'm not owning up to something. Like I'm pathetic. Like I have no control. I feel the worry I had for him slide slimily away, replaced with a thread of sulphur-red anger. I stop trying to help. '*You're* sick in the head. You've gotta get a grip.'

He shakes his head like it won't stop. 'I'm fine. Good. Never been better. You need to watch yourself. Diabetes is forever.' He points to the SOS bracelet that tells the world who I am. 'You're gonna be sick forever.'

'You don't get it, do you?' It's like there's fire in my eyes: they burn. '*I'm* under control but you're losing yours. If you don't watch it, you'll end up never able to get better. You'll go crazy, like Josh.'

He straightens suddenly. 'What would you know?' He grabs my shirt. 'You don't know shit about Josh. You never met him.'

The words fall out of my mouth. 'I knew he was mad.'

'He was not mad. He was not mad.' With every sylla-ble, he pulls at my shirt so I get closer and closer to him. 'He had an illness. He was sick. He couldn't help it. But I don't have it, Lewis. I'm the healthy one out of us.' He points to my wrist again but all I can see is how his finger is shaking.

I wrench backwards out of his grip and the pocket tears from my shirt. 'How do you know you're healthy?

You're not acting like it. Maybe you're getting sick. Sick like Josh. Mad. Crazy. Like your cousin.'

He takes a step back. 'I am nothing like Josh. You're a bastard, you know that?'

'At least I'm not a *mad* bastard.'

He doesn't say anything more but stares at me. We stare at each other but don't see. We're blinded by rage and the words that we've flung like spears. We stand so long that my eyes begin to clear and I see, written across his face in hollows and shadows, that I have accused him of the worst possible crime and he hates me for it. Hates me so hard and so strong that hatred feels like a living dangerous thing in his guts.

'In class, boys,' calls a teacher from across the courtyard, the voice sunny and uncaring.

We stand, unable to move.

'Right, boys. I mean now.'

There's no threat in anything a teacher could say at this very moment, nothing that would compare to what just happened, but our deadlock breaks as we both look towards the man. We stumble off in our own directions. I hear Bull's feet as he scuffs on gravel. It sounds like he's stumbling, shuffling, limping but I don't look. I go to the door of the building. I see Bull reflected in the glass. He's by himself, the teacher gone as soon as we moved. I see him walk crookedly out the school gate, slugging his way along the hot footpath, and I make no effort to stop him. I swing the door open, let it close behind me, shutting Bull, and his sickness, out.

29

BULL

How do you know you're healthy? You're not acting like it. Maybe you're getting sick. Sick like Josh. Mad. Crazy. Like your cousin.

I am nothing like Josh. You're a bastard, you know that?

At least I'm not a mad bastard.

Mad bastard, mad bastard, mad, mad, mad.

If I was confused before, I am shattered now. I walk for a long time, across town and back again. I walk through the Mall, across the footy field, along the edge of the creek. I'm panting by the time I get back to my place, parched because of the heat. I sit down in the kitchen, kick off my school shoes, and drink glass after glass of water.

After a long time, I cool down a bit. My cheeks are still inflamed; it's as if I'm allergic to the sun. I peel my shirt off where I sit and let it drop to the floor. My skin is sticky with sweat. I pull my shorts off next and sit in my jocks on the kitchen stool. Ella comes home looking just as hot but then she's been at tennis.

'Hey, Will,' she says, heading for the freezer and an icy-pole.

'El,' I say.

'Nice outfit.' She passes me on the way to her bedroom, and I hear her wardrobe door open and shut. She comes back out in a loose purple dress. 'Where's Sofie?'

'Arr shit.' I've forgotten Sofie. I walked the town but I didn't walk past her school.

'You've left Sofie at school?' Ella's eyes are popping. 'She'll be freaking out.'

'I'm going now.' I pull shorts back on and don't bother with the rest.

'I'm coming with you.'

We run out the door and into the heat. Instantly, I start sweating again. Ella runs easily beside me and I briefly wonder if we are really related. My body doesn't like running, it's not mechanically built for it. Next to Ella, I feel like an elephant lumbering along. My body is built for walking. Or maybe just standing. Definitely *not* running.

By the time we're a block away, Ella has left me way behind. I see my sisters sitting on the fence as I round the corner. Ella has an arm around Sofie. I pull up in front of them and lean my hands on my thighs to recover. 'Sorry, Sofie.'

'Did you forget me?' Her voice is small, sniffly.

'Well, I didn't really forget you. I just left school a different way.'

'You forgot me.'

I look into her dark eyes and see teary sadness. 'Were you okay here? Don't the teachers check that all the kids have gone home?'

'I didn't want anyone to know so I hid.' Sofie points to some bushes running along the fence.

'You shouldn't have hid, Sofie. It's better that the teachers know you're still here.'

'I didn't want them to know,' she repeats.

I shrug and offer her my hand but she's not that easily bought. She slips from the fence with Ella and takes her hand instead. 'Ella, I didn't want them to know.'

'I got it, Sofie,' says El. 'That's okay.'

'Do you know why?'

I'm walking a few steps behind them and can just hear what they're saying. Sofie's school bag bounces loosely on her back and I wonder idly whether I should take it from her.

'Why?' Ella's looking around her, probably checking whether she can see anyone that she knows to go and talk to.

'In case they think that Will's gone funny again.'

My footsteps slow right down. I'd thought that she was too young to remember. I couldn't get Sofie after school when you first left. Well, I could but I didn't always remember. I know it increased the pressure on Mum because she had to find someone else to do it. It was stupid because sometimes I'd get home from school and one of Sofie's friends' mothers would be dropping Sofie off at exactly the same time. Those mothers, they always had a hassled look on their faces. It was like seeing my mum mirrored in ten other mums.

So Sofie remembered all the fuss. See what you did? You stuffed around with her life too. My heart goes out to my little sister.

We trail into home, Ella leading, Sofie skipping behind her, me at the rear. Mum is home. I suddenly remember my shoes abandoned in the hall and my shirt on the kitchen floor. I brace myself for the onslaught but Mum's not in the kitchen. We find her flaked out on the couch, asleep in her work clothes. She has one arm on her stomach, the other flung over her eyes. I look at Ella. She looks back and puts her finger against her mouth to keep Sofie quiet. Together we move silently around the house, gathering up any bits and pieces that we'd left around. Ella feeds Sofie ice-cream and then we go to our rooms, leaving Mum in the tomb-like lounge.

My room is like an oven. I turn on the fan as high as it will go and lie on the carpet directly below it, arms and legs spread like a sand angel. I can see under my bed from here, with its shadowy fluff and abandoned muesli bar wrappers. My carpet is surprisingly soft and it's really pretty comfortable. I think of Sofie and smile. I think of Mum and frown. I think of Lewis and my head goes black.

You're getting worse. Like before. Sick, like before.

Forgetting Sofie doesn't mean I'm not well. It is not a sign. I'm definitely not sick like Lew. I can't work out why we're so wrong at the moment, so out of tune with each other. He's strange. Not himself. And yet he seems as normal as I've ever seen him. I'm not sure what's going on.

I stretch my legs out more and something crunches. I feel for it with my hand and come up with the genogram. Mr Henderson has moved onto another topic and I'm left with this sketch of my family. I sit up and smooth the paper out in front of me. My family. My roots. My heritage. They call it a family tree and I can see how the branches spread up and out from me.

I look again. No. The way that I've drawn this genogram puts me at the bottom so it's not a tree, it's a funnel. Everything is pouring *into* me. The faceless names of all my relatives point to me, drain towards me. I'm a mix of everything and everyone. A genetic soup that ends with me. Hazel eyes, long second toes, short curly hair. A pool of inherited traits that is me.

And what else is waiting for me? What disgusting sickness is lying dormant in my body ready to be released?

Your name and Great-uncle Len's bulge out of the page. Have I written them bigger than anyone else's? Should there be others that stand out as the mad, bad, black sheep of the family? Not on Dad's side, I've asked him. Mum's side? The only one that can tell me that is Mum herself. There's no other way of finding out, no amount of Googling that will help, no amount of second-guessing or wondering. I stand up holding the genogram, and leave my sweaty room. Mum is still asleep on the couch. I shake her awake.

'What?' Her eyes open wide, scared, confused.

'Mum,' I say. 'I need your help.'

She sits up quickly. 'What is it? Is Sofie okay?'

Ella comes in. 'Will, what are you doing?'

'Is Sofie okay?' Mum says, panicked.

Sofie runs in. 'I'm okay, Mum.'

'Oh.' Mum runs a hand through her hair. 'You woke me up, Will.' The confused look is still stamped on her face.

'Yes,' I say impatiently. 'I need your help.' I hold the paper out to her.

'That could have waited,' Ella says to me. 'Will. That could have waited.'

I shake my head. 'I need your help *now*, Mum.'

Mum rubs her eyes and looks at what I'm holding. 'I've already helped you with this, William.'

'I need to know who else.'

'What?'

'I need to know who else was like them, Mum.' I point at your name and Len's then take the pen and circle them. 'Who else was like them? Who else? Tell me.'

Mum is looking at me alarmed. She shakes her head but I know she's hiding something. 'Mum, I need to know. Who else?'

Behind me I sense, but don't see, that Ella and Sofie have gone stiff. Mum shakes her head again, quicker this time, so I rattle the paper at her. I'm getting angry. 'I need to know, Mum!'

'Will, don't.' Mum's voice is shaky.

'Mum. Come on.'

'Why do you want to know?'

'I need to know, Mum. I might be the same.' I rattle the paper again. It tears a bit in my grip. 'I might have it, too.'

She pulls back. 'You don't, Will.'

'But look!' I trace a line from Len to Josh to me. 'I could. I could get it. It's in the family.' I push the genogram at her and put a pen in her hand. 'Tell me. Who else?'

Her hand is shaking and I think for a moment that she isn't going to do anything. But then she lifts the pen up and circles one name. My Great-Grandma. Len's mother. The former owner of my piano. The person that played like a concert pianist. The true musical prodigy of the family. Mum drops the pen. 'Grandma Broadbent.'

The room is very quiet. I take the paper slowly from her, my eyes drawn to the new circle.

'It doesn't mean anything,' Mum says quietly. 'Grandma lived in tough times. There was war, depression, times were really bad for women. We don't know how these things affected people. We don't know their circumstances. We don't always know why people act like they do. Maybe she was just different from the rest of her family. Maybe it was her way of coping. Maybe if she was alive these days, she'd just be like the rest of us. This doesn't have any effect on you, Will.'

I'm not really listening. All I can see is the line winging down through the generations towards me. I have the answer I've been looking for. Slowly, I stand up. 'Thanks, Mum,' I say.

When I go to my room, I fold the paper roughly in half and put it away in a drawer. Someone knocks at my door but I don't say anything and no one comes in. The world is dark around me but I can feel the weight of my family history pressing hard and hot on my brain like a bright spotlight. So this is why I'm not getting better all these months after you died and left me. I'm going to be just like you, Josh. It's in my blood.

30

LEWIS

I don't know how the rest of the day went. I mean, I saw Charlie and Kendo kicking the footy after school. I saw Grace walking home, her open bag over one shoulder as if it weighed nothing. I saw Bonnie and felt my heart leap but could only watch as she leaned against the school fence to wait for her mum. I felt this yearning to just go and stand next to her, push my shoulder against hers as we stood with the wire fence pressing in our backs. I wanted to be in the same space as she was but I couldn't make myself move towards her. I wished she'd look up and see me, walk over, say 'Hi, what are you doing? Want to go somewhere with me? Want to just be with me?' Bonnie felt like a lifeline but I couldn't touch her.

The day disappears behind me.

I go home, straight to my room. My sketchbooks line up beside each other on my bookshelf. They're all the same except for the last one I bought. It seems slightly smaller than the others, the spiral back not as thick and black. It shits me. I pull my sketchbooks down and flip back through them until I find the picture of Bull as a whirlwind. I draw me as a carbon black tornado next to him and see how the lines clash and bash and destroy each other.

He's such a dick. *I'm* such a dick. How could we have said those things to each other?

I think about ringing him. Texting him. Whatever, just contacting him. I'm still angry, though – I think I might lose it again if he started on about me. And what I said – in part – was true. He *is* losing control; he *has* got to be more careful. I can see him un-ravelling even if he can't. The unfair thing is, can he stop it or does it have a will of its own?

When I got diabetes, the doctors kept asking whether anyone else in my family had it. But no one else in my entire family has ever had Type 2, let alone its evil parent - my nemesis - Type 1. Our families are about as fit as families get – a bit of cancer in the grandparents, some distant uncle who had a heart attack, and that's all. The doctors shook their heads but it didn't really make any difference. The fact was, *I* had it. Bad luck if no one else did.

Could having diabetes be as bad as what Josh had?

I shake my head. Comparing diseases is stupid. It's impossible, too, and I know that from being in the children's hospital where everyone's disease was terrible in its own way. It didn't matter if it was in your body or your head, or both. I remember the sobbing boy. Anyway, I can't think of what it means to be sick. I have to think *well* thoughts. I can't let Bull get me down, I can't think of what Josh might have been through. I take a big breath, set my armour in place and try to weld it on. Today, I'm focusing on me.

31

BULL

Hey, Bull, catch me. Catch me!

I wake up in the middle of the night sweating like a pig. The red hot dream evaporates from my body but I know it's been there, I feel it on my skin and in the way I don't know where I am – just for a moment – when I wake.

Catch me!

There are notes in my head, the running, scaling semiquavers of the chromatic étude. My fingers twitch, trying to get the fingering right. I sail through bar twenty-five and keep going, sliding up and down, faster and faster, until I sit up, stiff-backed, and hold my head.

———

I SEE GRACE. She flicks back her hair with her snake-adorned hand.

They were all tortured. Maybe the music did it to them.

I see Lewis. He looks sorry, then not, as he says, *you know, they say it's hereditary.*

I see Great-Grandma Broadbent sitting in a dark

picture theatre playing an old piano in the dark when everyone else has gone home.

Great Uncle Len drives his car too fast and wild.

Josh runs in front of me and shoots up that tree before I even make it to the park. *Catch me, Bull!*

I'M at the last bar, diminuendo. A big fat minim with a rest. For a brief moment, I hear nothing but the fading notes of the tune.

IF KURT COBAIN HAD LIVED, he would be old. With kids, maybe, or just living a rich man's life. Look what happened to Elvis. Got fat. Got ugly. Too many drugs. Maybe Kurt would weigh 150 kilograms by now, not able to move on the stage at all but hanging onto the microphone like he'd fall over without it.

Or would the music have left him?

Maybe there's a certain point where he would have been saved.

One day consumed by the fire of creativity; the next, working in a men's clothing store like Taylor. Hey, a customer would say. Don't I know you? Weren't you the guy...?

No, says Kurt. That was a long time ago. Pin stripes or plain grey?

Or maybe the music would have stayed but gone bad. Elton John-like. So new, so wild, in the first few years then blanded down for the rest of the world. Made more appealing for the masses. Sir Elton John, friend of many.

Or maybe Kurt would have seen what it was doing to him. He'd lived the exhaustion off the stage, the way the ordinary street lights prickled his eyes, the noise in his head from the clattering of constant notes. People thought it was drugs, but hell no, he was diseased with *music*. He'd had more sleepless nights with the sounds of songs trying to break free from his brain than he could take. He couldn't walk past a piano or guitar or a blank sheet of music score without trying out a new phrase, an old phrase re-vamped, even a single note. So he'd said, wait a minute, this life is driving me crazy. I'm going to stop. So he did. Cold turkey. And he'd lived.

WHEN PEOPLE TALK ABOUT CHOPIN, they say he was a gentle, shy man. They say his body was so weak with his sickness that he couldn't play the piano with any gusto. He couldn't do any 'big sounds.' He didn't like playing to large audiences. People describe his music as beautiful and noble, and perfectly structured. They say that you can't play Chopin unless you are in control of what you are doing because his music leaves no room for anyone to do it their way.

Everyone loves Chopin. In Poland, they named the airport after him. Before the war, Chopin was a symbol of freedom. His heart – in a jar filled with alcohol in some church in France – was hidden to protect it when Paris was bombed. Thousands play his compositions.

When I hear that chromatic étude, I can see the man that everyone loved. He's hooked over the keys, his head low, eyes closed, hands easily playing those technically brilliant pieces that he invented. I see the audience rapt in his playing. Some of them have their eyes closed. Some of them are tapping their thighs with their fingertips in a steady, rhythmical way.

But I can also hear his pain. His lungs are heaving with the physical effort of playing and inside his head, he's saying to himself *inside something gnaws at me*. People thought it was easy for him but it wasn't. When I hear Opus 10 number 2, I know all about Chopin and what he was really like. But it didn't – couldn't – stop him.

IF IT WAS my last day on Earth, the things I would do would be obvious. For instance, I would kiss Grace. I'd go right up to her, put my hands around her soft warm face and press my lips against hers. I wouldn't let her go until I'd felt the full thickness of her hair in my hands. And then I'd stop and walk straight away because, on that last day, there would be no room in my head for her to be angry or disappointed. I'd walk away imagining that the kiss was the best she'd ever had, was all she'd ever wanted, was her best last thing to do on Earth because it would be my best last thing.

If I had a week left on Earth, then I'd be more strategic. A week was a long time and I couldn't afford to stuff it up on the first day. Maybe I'd take things more slowly, savour the sight of Grace walking from one class to the next, drink a lot of Coke because in a week my teeth couldn't rot.

Maybe I'd spend six days planning for my last one and shower my family with gifts bought with any money I'd saved from working in that crazy fast food place. I'd give Dad an underwater watch and Mum a diamond necklace. Ella could have my guitar and Sofie could have the *Star Wars* Monopoly set Gran had given me for my thirteenth birthday. I'd eat chocolate cake for breakfast and hamburgers for lunch and whole fried chickens for dinner until finally the last day was gone and me with it.

But if I didn't know how long I had, only that it was going to be a shorter time than everyone else, maybe I'd start back-pedalling. Maybe I'd think, hey, if I look after myself I'm going to live longer. I'm going to stop smoking, drinking, drugs. I'm only going to eat crispy vegetables and wholegrain bread. I'll start jogging, join the gym, have my teeth cleaned. Stop swearing, stop lusting after Grace, stop hating Lewis for the things he said. I'm going to grab as much time as I can by any means that I have. I've gotta buy my time back.

If you knew you were going to die, you'd do anything to live. Wouldn't you?

———

Catch me.

———

The étude runs through my head again but distantly, softly. I let it run out and stop.

Then I give music up.

32

LEWIS

I draw. Lots. I keep myself busy. I am a busy, normal person.

I go back to Dr James. I sit and draw in the waiting room. Dr James runs late by an hour but I'm fine. I draw the room and the patient patients. Mum does a whole crossword, writes a shopping list and even steps out to make herself a hair appointment. Dr James comes to get me while she's gone and I sit by myself in her room, holding my sketchbook, feeling small, feeling big, while she looks at my toe and grunts in a medically satisfied way.

I do homework, even Maths, by myself. I think about Dad's promise and laugh. I don't ever get A's, not even in Art. Dad's safe. I could push myself and put things in on time or write more than two paragraphs for my essays but I don't. I do my homework but it's only just done. Just done enough to give me more time for drawing.

At school, I run to classes like everyone else to avoid the rain.

I draw Bonnie. Lots. I've started to look at her really

closely and can sketch the features of her face with no effort at all. She has clear eyes, and keeps them lined in black. Sometimes her mascara leaves tiny dots on her skin where her longest lashes touch it. She has three freckles in a cluster on her left cheek. Her teeth are braces-straight and she has a habit of feeling them with her finger, as if she can't believe how smooth they are. Her hair falls over that one eye but mainly I draw it hooked behind her ear so that I can spend more time getting the light right as it runs down to her chin.

What I don't do is think of Bull. Not even in slate grey.

'Party on Saturday,' says Kendo on a Monday. 'You'll be there.'

I'm on my way to the library. That's the other thing I've been doing. Libraries are great places to disappear in. 'Yeah,' I say and hold up a book like it's a bomb. 'Got to return this.'

'Great,' says Kendo, and does some sort of hip-hop move before he goes off to find Charlie. I feel a great raging jealousy at the way Kendo moves like he's choreographed everything he does. I go to the library, return my book, borrow another and sit reading it at a table. The bell goes. I walk out and join the rest of us going to class.

Out of habit, Bull and I sit together like usual.

He doesn't say one word. Not to me, not to anyone. I don't know where he goes at recess and lunch but it's not anywhere I am.

'Party tomorrow,' says Kendo on the Friday and I realize that another school week has passed.

Only Bonnie knows something's going on. I see her looking at me in class, looking at Bull, too, if he's there. She keeps her head slightly turned our way even while she's writing. I take in her long tanned legs bent under her chair and how she scoops her page as she writes in that tricky left-handed way. At one stage, she smiles at me. So small but so important to me. My face won't smile back but I know, once again, that she's keeping me grounded.

33

BULL

'William,' says Mum. 'I've had a phone call from Mr Sinclair.'

The television is loud and I try not to hear her. She's not fooled. She stands in front of it, facing me. I feel like I'm in front of a single person firing squad.

'Mr Sinclair is concerned that you're not going to orchestra practice anymore.'

I'm on the couch, exactly where the air conditioner hits. I've been there for an hour and have sunk low into the cushions. I like it. Maybe I'll sleep out here tonight.

'Mr Sinclair also said that you've missed two double bass lessons and haven't turned up for band practice for weeks.'

I'm not sure why Dad hasn't put more air conditioning units in this house. If he did, we wouldn't all fight for the couch when we want to watch the telly. His chair is right next to the couch and gets some cool air as well. Maybe that's all that matters to him. So selfish.

'And I also found this in the bin, among a whole stack of stuff you've thrown out.'

There's a really important bit in the movie coming up and it's essential that I see it. I peer around Mum, trying not to be too rude, but if I don't see this bit (even though I've seen it before maybe a dozen times) I won't understand the rest of the movie and there won't be any point in watching it.

'William!'

I look at her. Hard not to with that yell ricocheting off my face. She's holding a CD. My top 100. I mean, it used to be mine. I nod to show her I've seen it. I gaze back at the telly. She spins around and turns it off, spins back around to me. I sigh. Looks like I've lost the plot.

'Will, we need to talk.'

'Okay.'

'What's going on?' As if she suddenly realizes how confrontational she must look, she turns and plonks onto the couch next to me. On the edge of it, though. Her back is straight and her hands grip the CD tightly. 'Will, I see that you've put your guitar in its case.'

'Well, it doesn't get dusty that way.' I shake my head slightly. Isn't that what she's always telling me? Put the lid down on the piano. Put the covers on your instruments. Finally I do and she's cracking it?

'And I haven't heard you play the piano for weeks.'

I didn't know playing the piano was compulsory. I'm getting impatient now. Why is she telling me stuff I already know?

'Will, this isn't like you. Where's your music?'

I wince. The words have struck me like a slap. I try for some explanation that might do. 'I'm not interested anymore.'

Mum's puzzled. I've said the wrong words then. I think about some more but she gets in first. 'Why not?'

I'm sixteen, a kid. I don't have to stay interested in everything I try. 'Dunno,' I say.

She fiddles with the CD, turns it over and over. Despite myself, I watch the case because it doesn't close properly and if she isn't careful, it might fall out. But then I remember that I don't care anymore.

'Will, this has nothing to do with Josh, does it?'

Your name has a whole lot of stuff surrounding it so that when someone else says it, it's bigger than just four letters. Your name echoes in my head, bouncing around it like I've got an empty cavern for a brain. I wait for the noise to settle down and say, 'No. Josh didn't like music.'

Mum gets that look on her face again like she doesn't understand my sentence. 'But *you* like music, William. Don't give it up because of Josh.'

Now I don't understand her. This has nothing to do with you. This is bigger than you or me or even Mum. She doesn't get that I'm taking emergency action here. I'm being 'sensible' and 'reducing my risk factors' and all those things they cram down your throat about surviving being a teenager. Typical. When you do, the adults don't even recognize it. They think you're being 'unreasonable' and 'senseless.' I shake my head at Mum, irritated.

Mum smooths her hair back behind her ear, clears her throat, and does a quick look around the room. We're the only ones at home at the moment. We're trapped together. I have a sudden longing for Dad. He doesn't eyeball me like Mum. He lets me do what I want. Most of the time. He wouldn't be giving me the third degree over a CD I put together when I was sick. 'Well,' I say, 'better go and do some homework.' I leave the couch and walk into my room.

I don't know if I've got any homework or not but it doesn't matter because I won't be doing it anyhow. My room looks odd without pages of music on the floor. I've pushed the amp under my bed. The guitar is black in the corner. My music player is at the back of my sock drawer. It's a nothing-room now but it's safe. Nothing gonna get me now.

I open a book, read the first paragraph, forget what I read and read it again. Forget again. Shut the book. I see the journal that Mrs Mac gave us and pull it out from under three apple cores and two dirty mugs. I haven't done anything to it since it came my way. I open it now and see it full of blank pages. That seems to be right, so I take a pen and edge the page so that the white has a blue boundary. A photo frame of white. Safe faint blue lines run through the page, reminding me of school and what's in store for the next few years of my life. I think about looking at your notebook again but can't see the point. The stuff you put in there, that's not going to be me. You were writing a different life.

There's a crash at the back door as the rest of my family come home from the pool. I hear Sofie's high-pitched excitement. 'Guess what, Mum? Guess what Amy did? Guess what, guess what?'

What could be so interesting about a day in Grade 2?

'Got everything, El?' Dad asks.

'Yep.'

They go their separate ways.

El's door thunks closed.

Dad goes past my door, humming. He goes past again after a few minutes and I hear Mum call to him. They murmur from the lounge and I know it's about me because Mum is talking in that urgent, OMG way she has when a crisis is looming. Dad can't say anything until Mum's finished.

It's all a bit much, this listening and thinking. I crawl

into bed, suddenly exhausted. Dad comes in, as I knew he would, but he's too late. I don't want him there. I just need some dark time. He has other ideas.

'Come on, Will. We're going for a drive.'

'No thanks Dad.'

He pulls back my doona but I shoot my arm out and yank it up. He jumps in surprise. 'I need your help getting some stuff from the hardware store,' he tries.

'Take Ella. She's the fit one.'

'She's not big enough.'

'She's thirteen.'

'I mean, she's not big like you.'

'I'm busy.'

'You don't look it.'

I manage to stare at him. There's heat in my eyes. His go wide. 'Dad, I'm not going. I'm too tired, okay? Let me sleep.'

'Why are you tired? Big day at school?'

'Something like that.'

'If you sleep now, you won't sleep tonight.'

'Yes I will.' I'm sure about that. My body seems to be shutting down for a long rest.

Dad is quiet but he thrums his fingers on his thigh. 'Will, I'm not sure what to do.'

'Take El with you.'

'No. I'm not sure what to do with *you*. Did you have some trouble at school?'

Only with some unjust accusations. Sadness threatens to flood me. I push it away with Hulk strength. 'No.'

'I think it's time that you saw Mr Petersen again.'

Mr Petersen. He's a good bloke but I don't want to see him or his olive green office with its university degrees sticking on the wall. All I need, now that I'm in bed, is to sleep. I say so to Dad. 'I need to sleep. I think I have a virus.'

At this, Dad picks up. He looks at me almost eagerly. 'Have you got a sore throat? Headache?'

'Yes.' I have got a headache. I lie about the throat.

Dad nods. It all makes sense to him now. 'You do need to rest, then. Do you want anything, a drink? Headache tablets? Cough lollies?'

'No. Thanks.'

'Maybe you're getting the flu.' Now that I've given him something to grab on to, he's off and racing.

'Swine flu, probably.'

I've gone too far. Now he looks concerned again. 'Do you think?'

'Dad, I just need some sleep.'

'Right.' He stands up. 'Let's see what some rest does for you.' He goes out the door, shutting it carefully. I hear him say something to Mum and her answer him in the same tone as she'd used before. The virus thing doesn't have the effect on Mum as it did on Dad but it should put her off for a while. And really I need some sleep. I'm bone-achingly tired. Numbingly, crushingly tired. Maybe I really have got the flu.

I can fool Dad, I can nearly fool Mum, but I can't fool myself.

34

LEWIS

Kendo turns the lights down so that bodies are black silhouettes against the flashing walls of the room. I've got that image stored in my head for when I get home. I used to carry around a small sketchbook but it just didn't seem big enough in the end. Dancing people, girls together, boys draped against the speakers. I need a full A4 page to catch it, but sometimes I wish I had just *anything* to draw on. My fingers twitch.

Kendo's parties are famous. His neighbours hate him. His mother spoils him. She works weekends as a gaming assistant and gets home later than these parties finish. She's just glad he's having a good time. I think that Kendo has a gifted life and he doesn't bloody realize how good he's got it.

Bonnie's here. Jordan isn't. Her hair is down, hanging ruler straight to her shoulder blades in a shadow-wave. She has a top rimmed with sequins and they flash in the few lights that Kendo has left on. I swallow. Bonnie makes my mouth go dry.

I wish Bull was here. I'm glad Bull isn't here.

When I asked Kendo if he'd texted him he said that he hadn't got an answer. Then he'd asked me, 'What about when you talked to him?'

I shrugged.

How could I say, I didn't talk to him? Or, I did talk to him but it was the wrong way. I stop myself from thinking too much and flush rotten thoughts away with another cold beer. Kendo put one in my hand as soon as I got here, saying 'Saved you a few' but he must have saved us all a few. Charlie had his, so did Bryn and Steven and Doozy. This beer business is a strange take on Kendo's party – free beer isn't normal. Kendo winked at me as he handed it over. 'Don't worry, mate. Mum had a bit left over. Fortieth birthday last week.'

Yeah, I doubt that Kendo's mum would be so generous or so idiotic to let a bunch of teenagers drink beer without an adult present but who am I to argue? Good on you, Kendo's mum. Happy Friggin' Birthday.

Kendo walks off to turn the music up. I tear my eyes from Bonnie and go over to Charlie. We've used each other's houses as alibis. Partners in crime against the olds. We bash our cans together.

I'm staying at Kendo's party as long as I feel like. This is what everyone else does and this is what I'm doing tonight. I study the room. Grace is dancing with Jules, dark curls around her face. As I watch, she dances up to Charlie and takes his hand, leading him into the beat. He dances awkwardly, eyes on Grace. They grin and Charlie moves his hands onto Grace's waist. Jules puts her arms up and waves slender wrists back and forth. She yells out the chorus. Grace joins in with her eyes closed and her head flung back. Charlie keeps dancing, pulling Grace closer so that his hips bump hers.

'They look pretty good together.'

I nearly step away from the voice in my ear but realize in time that it's Bonnie leaning in to make me hear. Her arm touches mine and I feel my skin turn hot.

I drink, knocking back the can.

'I didn't think you…' Bonnie looks at me, pulling her hair back behind her ears but it doesn't stay. I lift my hand to help her but it has an empty can in it.

'Should you be…?'

I scowl. 'I can do what I want.'

Bonnie flushes, I can see that even in the dim light. 'Sorry. I didn't mean to…'

'Well, I'm fine. I'm right and good and normal. Right and good and normal.' And I don't seem to be able to shut up. 'Right and good…' Bonnie backs off.

The song changes. It's hard and thumping. I want Bonnie to stay but can't think how to keep her there and it's a relief when Jules comes up to me, and puts a slender hand on my shoulder. 'Dance, Tall Man!'

That's what they call me at the height of Kendo's parties.

I answer by striding into the dance scene and doing a sort of long-legged scramble that makes Charlie whoop and whack me on the shoulder. Fuelled by beer, I dance long and hard, with and without Jules, until Kendo finally turns the music off. I look around and only see Charlie and Grace still there. Where's Bonnie? Where did she go? I need to talk to her.

The lights come on. Kendo starts to pick up empty cans.

Normally, I would help. The rubbish, though, seems a long way away. I sit on the couch and watch as Grace scoops things up and into a black plastic bag. It doesn't take long. Ten people don't make a huge mess. Kendo straightens the blanket on the back of the couch and you could swear, if you couldn't smell the sweat and hormones in the air, that there hadn't been a party here at all. 'Better open the windows, mate,' is my only contribution. Kendo nods and does it.

Charlie has one last look around but doesn't appear to see anything left to do. 'Well, we're going.' He hoists me up. 'What about you, Grace?'

In that milli-second when Charlie looks only at Grace and Grace pauses to think about what's been said, I have a heart-sink. Don't, I think at Grace. Please. For Bull's sake. Don't do it, Grace. Don't hurt him like I just did.

Grace makes up her mind. She smiles slowly, twists curls around her finger. 'I'll ring my dad. He'll come to get me.' She's wearing a short black skirt with stockings ripped from knee to thigh. I can't seem to stop looking. She has drawn a crucifix on her skin along the rip.

Charlie is looking, too. I think he's drooling. At last he shrugs, his eyes suddenly downcast, his face dark red in the lounge room light. He pushes me roughly until I start moving. 'Okay. See you later then.' He pushes again, making me stumble.

We stagger out the door into the muggy night, my stomach suddenly churning. The street is quiet and our footsteps seem to slap loudly on the footpath. It's not that late, probably only midnight, but I feel like the day has ended. 'I'm going to go home to my place.'

'Sure?' says Charlie, sounding tired.

'Yes.'

We separate at the corner. Charlie puts his hands in his pockets and disappears into the shadows of the night. I start walking the ten blocks to home, feeling the path hard under my danced-out feet. The sky is indigo with storm. I hear thunder in the distance and am suddenly scared of being alone under the intensity of that thick sky. As if to mock me, lightning flares in the sky and shows me a glimpse of the thunderheads above. The club is ahead and I feel better as I step into its glaring outside light.

It happens in slow motion.

I am walking towards the entrance. A man and a woman come out in front of me. I walk further into the light. They go into the shadows of the driveway. I automatically watch them as I go, not really caring who they are. They turn to each other. I see my Dad. He doesn't see me. He stretches his arm out to the woman and pulls her into a kiss. I don't see Mum. I keep walking away.

My heart is pounding in my alcohol-stupefied body. I'm in the shadows of the footpath and turn back to see what they are doing. Dad runs his hands down the woman's back and onto her bum. I feel really sick. A sudden thought explodes into my head – is this *Max*? Dad's mate Max? What about *Mum*?

I start to run home, wobbly and flat-footed. I don't look back. Dad beats me there, though. His car tick ticks in the carport as I reach the back door. I pull it open but quietly, afraid again. I see Mum in the kitchen, Dad nodding to her as he goes past to the bedroom. She knows, I can see the look on her face. She's always known.

I wait until she flicks the light off and goes to bed before sneaking into my room. I must have made some noise though. I'm sitting on my bed peeling off my shirt when Mum puts her head into my room and says, 'You okay?'

'Jesus, Mum!' I says, covering my scrawny chest with my shirt. 'Yeah, I'm fine.'

'Not staying at Charlie's?'

'I felt like coming home.'

She nods. From the bedroom, Dad snores like he's worn out.

I look at Mum but her face is blank. 'See you in the morning.' She shuts my door gently.

I lie down and pick up my sketchbook in one nauseous motion. I start drawing but the scene dwindles. Defeated, I put the book on the floor. The whirling night is in my head and I can't sleep. I see Dad. I see Mum. I see them staying together because of me. Finally, hours later, sleep comes, as dark as the building storm.

THE MORNING COMES TOO early and with crushing sound and light. Magpies fight with their children just outside my window, screeching unhappily. Their angry fluttering makes shadows on my curtains and it's probably that, rather than the morning light, that has woken me up. I groan, pull my doona around my ears, feeling sweat ooze out and be soaked up by the cotton cover.

I can't think of Dad. I can't.

Another thirty minutes of lying there makes no difference to how I'm feeling. Nausea still rolls in my stomach, threatening me with action if I move too fast. How many beers did I end up having? My head is thumping lightly, another warning. My skin crawls with fatigue and a shadowy something that reminds me of those many times that I've been sick.

No. I'm not even thinking about it. I am *better*. I have not been sick for weeks and I'm not going to start now. The shadowy something drifts into my head and tries to smother my thoughts. I close my eyes and try to breathe it away.

Another thirty minutes goes past and The Judge is at

the door, knocking softly at first and then more firmly. I say, 'I'm fine, Mum,' but she knows the code and so comes in straight away. She moves towards the blue bag on my desk but stops. 'Is there something you need to do now?'

I know what she wants me to do. I also know that she's trying not to do it for me. This is just one morning in the rest of my life and I have to show her that she doesn't have to be knocking on my door every single day. But I hesitate. She could do it so easily, unzip that bag and take out the monitor. Jab my finger for me. It would be so easy…

No. I struggle up, swallowing against the rising vomit, squinting with my head pain. *Why aren't you angry?* I think at her before I can stop myself. *Why are you putting up with it?* I shake my head, and regret it. 'I'm up now,' I say as well as I can between clenched teeth.

Mum rocks on her feet but makes the decision to go. She doesn't shut the door fully, though. The crack lets through radio noise and the domestic whirring of the washing machine. I stand up slowly and get the bag, sitting back down on the damp doona. My fingers are shaking as I prick my finger, dab the scarlet blood on the machine, and wait. The final beep shows me what I don't want to know and I counteract with a jab to my stomach.

SOME HOURS LATER, I'm sitting on the couch staring out to the garden where Mum weeds vigorously in a sombrero-like gardening hat. I had thought she was The Judge of this house, She Who Rules. I was so wrong, this whole *thing* is so wrong. I feel unbelievably sick. The shadowy thing has passed right through my body and stripped away the good feelings of the last week. It has coloured my body delft blue, the same colour as the continuing storm clouds gathering again for their fight. I'll always be here, you know, it says. Don't push it.

Don't push it. Don't think you're normal. Don't think you can act normal.

Nothing is normal any more.

I. Hate. My. Life.

A WHOLE DAY and a night have gone by with me refusing – *refusing!* – to let myself sink back to where I was. *Listen, body. I'm in control.* I get my bike lock and bash myself hard on the leg. Crap, it hurts. A lump rises on my shin – I can see it get bigger - and I imagine the blood oozing then congealing under my skin. That will be a huge, thick, stormy bruise by lunch time. *You see?* I say to my body. *You cannot keep doing this to me. I'm in control here.*

I ride to school and park the bike in its usual position. Kendo is here already, his BMX covered in mud from the sudden torrential rain we're having that wreaks havoc on the dirt edges of the roads. Charlie gets driven to school by his mum who works not far away. Bull? Well, he walks with his sisters. He'll be here already. Yeah.

Kendo says it first. 'Where's Bull?'

'Dunno. Why?'

'Can't see him anywhere.'

I shrug as if this is normal. It could be. Bull has to wait for the girls and if they're running late, then he will too. Something tugs at me sharply - black guilt deep inside.

Charlie's next. He starts to say, 'Where's B-?' but stops like the words have fallen out of his mouth. Grace and Bonnie are in sight. They come over and stand with us and are soon joined by Jules. 'Great party, Kendo,' says Grace and smiles vixenly in Charlie's direction.

Charlie steps towards her.

'Glad to be of service.' Kendo does a small bow then straightens. His shirt strains against his torso and Jules giggles.

'Where's Bull?' says Grace, stepping back from Charlie, and I rack up three. 'He wasn't there on Saturday.' She looks at me, stares at me, knows about me.

'He'll turn up.' This is Kendo. So sure of everything. 'He'll be around.'

'Are you okay?' Bonnie says to me. 'You look sort of tired.'

'Couldn't sleep,' I say honestly. 'Too excited about coming to school.'

Bonnie nods uncertainly and I want to take her fingers in mine. Everyone else laughs. Jules tosses her hair and combs its long blonde strands with her fingers. Kendo crosses his arms, bulging forearms taut. I have a sudden vision of what we'd all be doing if it was still holidays. We'd be at the pool, spending all day lying around under the shade sail talking about harmless shit and not worried by anything. Well, that's not strictly true. Over the holidays there were bad spots as well. Jules came to the pool crying one day and wouldn't let us know why. Kendo spent two whole days refusing to talk to anyone. Everyone has things going on. It's just ordinary life.

The bell goes. I pick up my school bag. Ordinary life. What is that again?

I'M FINALLY DRAWING Saturday night. Not the club. Kendo's. Dancing shapes press themselves into walls. Beer bottles line the table. Jules thrusts her hips at Kendo. Charlie and Grace are one shadow, joined together in a tangle of arms, legs and hair. Bonnie is there alone and I'm nowhere to be seen.

I put the notebook down. My fingers are suddenly tired, the dark pencil feels loose in my grip. I throw it across the room and it hits the wall with a tink and falls onto the carpet. It's not yet five o'clock in the morning but I'm wide awake even though I've hardly slept. The heat is already thick and the air feels odd, full of electricity. I pull the curtains apart and all I can see is grey sky. The sun dares not rise today. Chicken.

It's a bit early, but I do my testing. Sky high. A sudden red cloud falls over my eyes and I squeeze them shut tightly. What is going on? I do one thing wrong – have one normal night with my mates - and I'm up shit creek? Not fair. Not fair at all. I give myself some extra insulin and then worry it's too much and think about carbs to balance it all out.

Mum hears me stomping around the kitchen and comes out in her pale blue dressing gown bleary-eyed. I see her always there, always there for me. 'Hey,' she says, leaning on the bench. 'What's up?'

I show her my record book and then go back to making scrambled eggs. I've got the frying pan too high and the eggs burn a bit. I pile them onto toast that's only half cooked and take the soggy mess to the table to eat. Mum sits down next to me, running her finger down my list of figures, checking my BGLs against my dosages. 'It's been so good.'

'Yeah,' I says, egg falling from my mouth. There's a moment of silence then I slam my knife down on the table. 'Yeah! That's exactly right.'

Mum watches the knife as it wobbles to a stop. 'Lewis, you know that this sometimes happens. It has before.'

'I know.' The fork joins the knife and knocks it along

the table. 'It's shit, Mum. This is shit.' I don't just mean my diabetes.

She does her best not to look startled but I know she is. I don't crack it, I never have before. Not to her. This is new stuff to her. It's not to me because I've said it inside my head heaps of time before. It's just never made it to the outside world. Mum finally gets some words out. 'Now, Lewis. We've got through it before. Maybe something happened at the party? Did something happen?'

Oh, yeah, something happened all right.

She knows what I did. She would have smelt me a mile off when I came home. Why doesn't she come right out and say it? I should have gone to Charlie's. Then I wouldn't have…I don't think anymore, stopping myself by folding the bread in half and cramming egg into my mouth.

I wish Mum would go back to bed. She really doesn't get it. I don't want *us* to get through it. I don't want to have you help me, Mum. I don't want to *need* you to help me. I want to work things out for myself and do what I reckon should be done, including whether or not I should have got pissed on Saturday. I don't want anything to do with her at the moment. I'd thought she was The Judge, *in control*.

Mum is waiting for me to say something or nod my head or do whatever it is I usually do in these situations to show that I've fully understood the consequences of my actions.

When the plate is empty in front of me, I lean back in my chair with my hands behind my head and my eyes closed. Mum leans towards me so that as I tip forwards again and open my eyes she's suddenly right there. In my face. I shove the chair back and stand up.

'I've got to get ready for school.'

The clock in my bedroom says 5.55am. I have two

hours and thirty-five minutes to get ready for school. Sometimes, there's too much time in my life. Despite this, I get to school five minutes late. It's like I've never been anywhere else.

I don't see the others until the beginning of lunch-time and they catch me before I make it back to my locker.

'Where's Bull?' says Kendo and his words echo in my head. I don't say anything until Charlie says, 'Yeah, where's Bull?' He looks at me.

'Why should I know? I'm not his goddamn keeper.'

That was a mistake. Jules puts her hand to her mouth. Kendo gapes at me. Charlie frowns. Grace goes white. But Bonnie, no. Bonnie's looking at me as if I'm a turd. I see myself through their eyes - wild, red-eyed, frothing-at-the-mouth Lewis.

'I just mean,' I try to explain, 'that I don't know where he is every minute of the day.'

'What's going on?' says Bonnie slowly. 'What have you done?'

'Me? What have *I* done?'

'Why isn't he at school? He wasn't here yesterday, either.'

I feel slightly crazed that she even noticed that Bull wasn't here. 'If you're so interested, why don't you ask *him*?'

The bitterness in my voice makes Charlie shake his head but it's too late, I've spoken and without saying anything incriminating, they see my guilt blaze.

'You know he isn't over Josh dying,' Kendo says. 'You have to be careful what you say to him. He blames himself.'

Jules shakes her head. 'Why would Bull blame himself?'

Charlie gives her a hard look. 'He was chasing Josh. Josh was running around and Bull was trying to stop him.

Instead, Josh went up the tree and fell. Bull thinks that he wouldn't have done it otherwise.'

There's silence as we take that in. I feel rotten.

'So,' Kendo says finally, slapping me on the back, 'leave him alone.'

'Why are you all blaming me? I didn't do anything to him.' But they don't believe me. They can hear the lies in my voice. 'He was the one accusing me of being sick!'

Kendo and Charlie look at each other. 'Time to go,' says Charlie and hoists his sports bag up on his back. They leave without a backward glance at me.

'Come on, Bon,' says Grace, following Jules as she goes after the boys, but Bonnie stands there still, looking at me.

I look at her but find it hard to meet her eyes. I settle for those chocolate-coloured freckles. After the longest ten seconds of my life, I say, 'I didn't mean to, Bonnie, but he makes me feel sick when I'm not. I don't need that.' I catch her eye and see her staring at me. 'I've got to keep myself going. That means that sometimes I don't have room for Bull.'

She doesn't say anything for the longest time, even after the bell goes and we're still standing there, me with my head bent over like a green stick. I think she's bowing down with me when she suddenly pulls herself up and straightens. 'I know,' she says in the softest of voices. 'But it's possible that we'll never get over it, you see.'

Her voice is so rich in pain that I drop my books on a seat and take her hands instinctively. She clutches at mine and we fold them together so hard it hurts. 'I'm so sorry, Bonnie,' I say, the warmth of her skin burning mine.

She bends over again, her ponytail swinging over her left shoulder. Our hands are wet with her tears so I hang on harder. 'Lew,' is all she can say.

'I can't do the rest of today, Bonnie.' My voice is gone,

I'm only whispering. 'I can't.' My head swims with images I can't stop.

'I know a place we can go.' She doesn't look up. 'Come with me.'

We slip away.

35

BULL

I stay in bed for four days, except, of course, to go to the loo. I don't cough or sneeze even once so it's pretty obvious that I haven't got the flu.

'Hey, Will. Getting up yet? Feel okay now? Ready for the day?'

Dad comes in a lot. He doesn't knock. He sits on my bed and looks out the window. The weight of his body almost tips me onto the floor but I don't seem to have the energy to either fall or stay. My body ends up rolled towards his, jammed up against his solid thighs. Dad doesn't say much but his face is droopy and sad.

'Hey, Will, ready yet?'

As I watch his face, there's a twitch in the corner of his left eye. When he leaves, I roll-flop back the other way.

Ella comes in and roams my room restlessly. She talks at me, not pausing to let me answer even if I had wanted to.

'Will, this is really stupid. Mum's going crazy. She's cleaning non-stop and spending all day in the kitchen and she won't go to work. It's horrible. And she hardly talks to us. I need you to get up. Go on, get up.'

I can't tell her that it's impossible because I'm not in control yet.

Sofie drifts in and out. She brings me her teddy bear and then her giant stuffed dog. She settles them in the bed beside me and I sweat on them but she doesn't mind. She keeps up a rattle of talk for the sake of her toys.

'Will needs a lot of sleep at the moment, Teddy. He needs to do a lot of thinking, Mum says. Remember when this happened before? He got better. Mr Petersen helped him. We helped him. He's going to be better soon.'

I hope she's right.

Mum stands at the doorway but can't seem to come any closer.

I don't tell them about the nights. At night, I can sit up. I move around my room as restless as a little kid. I stand at the window, rocking on my feet, and stare outside. I watch possums sneak across the power lines and fruit bats wing past. It's so quiet here at night. The quiet seems to help me. I breathe easier, my shoulders relax. It's only the days that seem to worry me, the busy days full of noise and activity and *speed*. I don't want speed, I want slow. I just want a bit of time.

On Tuesday, I hear Mum on the phone talking to the doctor. I listen to the strategies they're working on, most of which I know of from before.

'Yes, green vegetables.'

'Yes, regular sleep pattern.'

'Yes, lots of exercise and get going with normal activities.'

I could tell them stupid strategies like that aren't going to work because this is something I've inherited. No cure for this, you see. It's drained into me from above. It's hopeless, people, hopeless. I lie in bed and listen, sick of bed but not yet ready to join in again. I think that they'll cram spinach into me the moment I get up. I guess that they'll join me up to the gym. I worry that they'll want me to play my music.

They might have been about to start some of their carefully made plans, but in the afternoon the storm starts.

I have no warning. I haven't seen any weather forecasts for days. Although my blinds are open, to me the sky is grey every day. Colour has gone from my world. When the rain starts in earnest, I listen to its pounding with a sort of hypnotic want. It gives me a noise to concentrate on that isn't the beat of Pinprick drums in my head.

When the power goes out, I don't notice that either. I haven't needed power for four days. I haven't really needed power for weeks. The noise grows louder and I gradually realize that something is wrong. The noise is louder than it should be, even for a summer storm, even for the sort of giant storms that have been tearing at us all summer.

I sit up, push back the doona, swing my legs over the edge. As well as rain, there is a hooshing, crashing sound of wind intent on doing damage. This storm is yelling at us that it's dangerous.

Mum appears in my doorway. I look at her. She is clutching the door frame, looking at me but also out the window. 'I'm going to get the girls.' She is gone out of sight almost as quickly as she appeared. When she opens the door to leave, the noise outside tries to get in. She shuts it out with her.

My night restlessness skyrockets into day jitters and pushes me out of bed. Out of my room. I walk into the lounge so that I can look at the street. The noise is just as bad here. Waves of water are falling from the sky and trees are bent double with the stress. Even the power lines are moving freakily, swinging like dangerous skipping ropes completely out of sync with each other. The gutters are full, water sheeting down onto the ground. I've never seen anything like this. The back of my neck prickles. The rain teems down. The wind smashes it around. One moment I can see out of the window, the next it's covered with a wave of water. I wait for it to break the glass. I think I even see the window bend inwards a bit.

Strange sounds start inside. I prowl the house and discover water running down the bathroom wall. More drips from the light fitting. I put a bucket underneath and start an intense investigation of every room. There's water in Mum and Dad's room and I pull their bed out of the way and put a towel on the carpet to catch the waterfall. Rain runs under the back door. I stopper it with an old jumper of Dad's. The lounge room seems relatively dry except for the condensation starting on the windows but then I see disaster looming. Plaster is beginning to sag in the corner over the piano. If it caves in, the piano will be drowned.

Great-Grandma Broadbent's piano, all the way from England on a ship, about to be drowned. On another day, the irony of that would make me smile but I'm not in a laughing mood. The piano stands against the inner wall of the lounge, just where pianos are meant to stand. In the dull light, its golden-brown surface is plain brown. Mum keeps the candlesticks that slip into its front runners in the linen press. We've never used them. I imagined that Great-Grandma did, maybe all the time. Perhaps this was the piano she'd used in the movie theatre and the candles were the only light she had. Maybe she played until they burned down to nothing. Maybe she kept playing in the dark. My strange great-grandmother, playing tunes to the possums and the bats.

The plaster slips a bit and a trail of water dribbles out. I've got seconds to make a decision. Save the piano? But I don't play anymore. But is that the point? Just because *I* don't, does that mean I *shouldn't* save it? Shouldn't I be saving it for the rest of the family? Saving it in the memory of Great-Grandma, no matter what she was like?

Mum has probably been away for an hour. In that time, the storm has come inside the house. It's trying to match the storm that seems to be continually raging in me. But the outside storm I can fight. The inside one…

Water pulses through the crack. More plaster sags.

I make up my mind. I'm going to defend the piano, defend my clever Great-Grandma who played like a concert pianist.

I get my body behind it and push. Who said that being bulky wasn't good? I get stronger the more I push. Blood flows through my body and I'm warm, hot, with the movement. Slowly, the piano wedges away from the wall. I swap sides and heave again. Just as I get the whole thing away from the corner, the plaster gives way with a soppy whoosh and water pours through the roof. I keep pushing the piano, jamming the old thing hard against the couch.

With the hole in the ceiling, the noise from outside is worse. The water keeps pouring through. I jump over the couch and empty the kitchen bin on the floor before jamming it under the flow. Water soaks into the carpet but the piano is safe. The initial flood through the hole slows to a steady but small stream. Just to make sure, I shove the piano once more until it tips the couch up. The lamp wobbles and falls, bouncing onto the cushions and miraculously surviving. I grin like a maniac. The lounge room is doomed but the piano and the lamp are alright.

All that heaving and shoving must have shot some adrenalin into me. I feel so unexpectedly good that it takes me a while to realize that the house is getting darker as more clouds arrive at the party. I dance a bit around the back of the piano but stop when thunder crashes somewhere close. The sound of running water is coming from the street. It's louder than the actual rain.

For the first time, a small thread of fear trembles its way along my body. The adrenalin is oozing away but leaves my heart pumping hard and my muscles warm. I take action and empty the bucket in the bathroom down the bath, putting it back where it had been. I swap sopping towels over with dry ones. I get another of Dad's jumpers and jam it under the front door. I manage one glance outside and see the street flowing like a river. There's no sign of Mum. There's no sign of anyone.

Terrible thunder shakes the house. I feel the storm directly above me, confirmed by simultaneous lightning flashes. The sudden light doesn't help me see – it's too quick and the water reflects it blindly. I find a torch and continue my vigilante stance against the weather, the storm, my imagination. The thunder is making me nervous – it's so loud and so often - but I keep swapping buckets and towels. The lounge room bin fills quickly and I use a big saucepan in its place to give me time to empty it.

I don't know how long I do this. The darkness thickens and by the time I sense that the rain is easing, it's almost night. Hours have passed, then. I'm still alone in the house. I open the front door and shine the torch outside. Water is pouring angrily down the street and there's not a sign of any traffic or people or animals. I shut the door again to keep the wind from pushing rain into the hall.

When nothing has changed after another half an hour, I try the phone. The land line is dead and my mobile reception is nil. In the drawer in the laundry, I find a battery operated radio and fumble to find spare batteries.

At last I get a news broadcast which gives sketchy news of widespread storm damage and flooding. No kidding, I think. I put the radio in the middle of the coffee table and turn it up as loud as it will go. The static drowns out the rain but not the thunder. My torch is slowly dying so I flick it off unless I'm checking buckets.

The gap between lightning and thunder gradually increases, so slowly it takes a while to notice. The storm loosens its hold. I shine the torch again out the front door and see that although the rain is still falling, it's no longer in sheets. I go back to stand in the lounge with one hand on the piano. I'm defending my house. Something stirs in me, something that's been missing the past few days.

I feel like *me*.

36

LEWIS

We walk away from school into the building heat of the day. I start sweating. When I glance at Bonnie, she has a sheen to her face that I'd like to draw. We walk through the streets to the edge of the bush, and start up the gravelly track. I'm not sure where we're going because I've only ever driven past this road. Bonnie seems sure, though. She walks slightly in front of me, her arms swinging. We've left our stuff at school so we walk quickly, our feet making scrunching sounds on the loose stones.

It probably takes half an hour before we get to the creek. I don't know the time because I've left my phone in my bag at school. The day is getting darker with more and more storm clouds but it could have only been mid-afternoon. We stop at the creek and watch its trail of dirty water.

'We've had a lot of rain this week,' says Bonnie softly. 'I've never seen it running before.'

'How often have you been here?'

She shakes her head. 'Not very often. Mainly with Josh.'

The water carries leaves and small sticks with it. I watch them catch on the edge, swivel around, be swept away. I didn't know Bonnie with Josh, only with Jordan. 'You still miss him.'

Bonnie shakes her head but then answers, 'Yes. I mean, I think I do. It went so wrong in the end.'

I look at her but can't see any tears. Instead, she's frowning at the water. Before I can say anything, she jumps to the other side, one foot sliding into the mud. I jump as well but my long legs make it easily. I catch her mid-slide and pull her up.

'Thanks!' Her hair has stuck to her forehead so I push it out of the way of her eyes. Her skin is clammy. 'It's this way.' She points and we walk on. My hand is still caught in hers.

The track goes up a hill. By the time Bonnie points again, we've left the creek behind around the corner. Thunder rolls. Rain begins to fall in slow, huge drops. Through the trees to the right I can see a dark shape that could be a tangle of shrubs.

'What is it?'

'It's Josh's hut.'

'He made it?'

'No. It was already here.' She steps off the track and I follow her. The rain is falling more quickly and wet leaves slap on my face as I push through the bush. We walk about fifty metres, stepping over stones and stumps and sticks. As we get close, I can see that the dark shape is a hut. It's made out of rough tree slabs and a shrubby roof sits crookedly on top. One push and maybe the whole thing would go over. Bonnie steps up to it and goes through an open doorway on its side. I step in after her.

The summer rain has left the hut with a floor full of puddles but someone has made a long seat out of logs at the back. Bonnie sits down, leans against the rough wall then crosses her arms in front of her and rocks forward slightly. 'What do you think?'

I sit beside her and nod. I can see why Josh might have liked coming here. Inside, it's harder to notice the crooked lean of the walls. It feels safer. The rain comes through the roof but only in small drips. I can see where water has come under the walls but, at the back on the logs, Bonnie and I are fine.

'I've been here a few times by myself.' Bonnie puts her head down. 'After Josh.'

'Did you ever come here with Jordan?'

'No way. Never with Jordan.'

I like the way she answers so quickly, with real fire in her voice, then I feel stupid for saying it in the first place. 'Sorry.'

'No, it's okay. Jordan was a mistake. My mistake. But at least I didn't bring him here.'

I feel huge relief and smile.

She sighs and unwraps her arms. I turn to her and she suddenly leans in to me, her lips finding my mouth. We kiss – hard, desperate kisses that feed an earthly longing that I've probably been carrying ever since I'd known her. I feel her teeth under my lips, her hair in my mouth. When we stop, I'm panting like I've run a race. We do it again, gentler, deeper, and I feel like I could faint. My hands cling to her warmth. I can hear thunder but it's so distant I wonder whether I'm dreaming.

The rain gets heavier and the roof drips turn to a heavy dribble. I lean too far forward and it pours onto my head. I laugh and pull away from Bonnie. She laughs, too. The happy sound makes me laugh more and some of the bitterness of the last few days dilutes. We come back together, wrap arms around each other. Bonnie's breath is on my neck as she rests her head on my shoulder.

'I did try hard with Jordan,' Bonnie says, and stops. After a while she adds, 'He was so…'

I wait for her to say what I had always thought. Jordan was tough and strong. Indestructible. Solid, dependable-

'…weak.'

This surprises me but I let her think over what she's just said. In the moments that it takes her to say anything more, the wind picks up.

'He just didn't want to understand. He thought Josh was past history for me, that *Jordan* was going to be the answer to all my problems.'

I nearly tell her about what I saw that day in the park but don't want to sound like I'd been spying. I remember Jordan looking out over the empty swings. It makes me suddenly angry – a scarlet flash – but then I think again. 'You probably think I'm weak as well.'

I've said it softly but she turns on me like I've shouted.

'What are you talking about?'

'You know.' I turn the bracelet on my wrist without thinking about it. She looks but doesn't understand. I tap it. 'The diabetes.'

'Oh.' Her voice is surprised. I'm surprised at her surprise.

'Don't you?'

'Think you're weak because you've got diabetes?' Now she's scowling. 'What sort of person do you think I am?'

'I didn't mean anything about you.'

'Well, it sounds like it.' She sits up and pulls away. 'You didn't ask to have diabetes, just like Josh didn't ask to have bipolar. It's part of you, isn't it? What would make me think that something you can't help would make you weak? You're just being an idiot, Lewis Pascoe.'

'I can't help it, you're right. But…' I think about what I'm trying to say. 'It's the sort of thing that even if you do everything the doctors' tell you, sometimes it goes all wrong.'

'Yeah, well, I know about that.' Bonnie ducks her head and grasps her hands together. I watch her twist her fingers and rub at the skin. I put my hands on her. 'Josh tried,' she said softly. 'He did. The counselling was alright but the medication was horrible and he couldn't stand it so he stopped.' She looked up at me. 'I don't know what I would have done if I'd been him.'

I shake my head because I don't know what I would have done either. We sit and listen to the angry wind lashing at the old hut.

'Jordan was weak, Lew.' Bonnie looks up at me and puts her arms around my neck. 'He had no excuse. You and Josh? I don't think either of you were weak at all.'

She can't know how much her words mean to me. I think of all those times I've spent away from school, in hospital, at the doctor's, thinking that they made me someone that people pity. But I also remember how the guys at school just pick up where we leave off whenever I get back, nothing changes, no big deal. Bonnie's words are like a torch and I can suddenly see.

I start smiling at her but there's a howl like a deranged wolf and the wind surrounds us.

'Water,' says Bonnie. We unravel and move our feet back, away from the brown water coming in under the walls and travelling towards us in a murky brown line. More water streams through the walls where the wood has slipped or rotted. I think I see the roof begin to sag.

'Maybe we should go,' I say.

'We'll get really wet,' says Bonnie.

'We're going to anyway.'

There's a crash outside. I jump up and look through the doorway. A tree is down about twenty metres away, its leaves bent and battered against the rain. Other trees wave wildly and the sky darkens further. I've drawn tornadoes but what do they actually look like in real life?

Bonnie comes to stand beside me. 'God, it's awful out there.'

'I don't think we can go anywhere at the moment.'

She nods. 'It won't last long. Will it?'

'I don't know. It might.'

We go back to our log seat, no longer talking because the noise outside is too much. Just the rain belting down is noisy enough but the wind is gusting, pounding against the old hut and making branches snap. Thunder cracks. Bonnie puts her head down and covers her ears with her hands. I keep looking at the roof, wondering how long it's going to stay on.

It gets worse. More rain, heavy and sideways. More wind, gusts joining together so it screams in a language I've never heard. A piece of roof peels off and snaps away, exposing the burnt umber sky. We shrink together, my taller body a cave over Bonnie's. I try not to think of Jordan's elbows pinning her to the ground. The ground is soggy under our feet.

It goes on and on. In the quieter moments, I say, 'Bonnie?'

'It's okay,' she says. The wind kicks up again and flattens our words.

At one stage, I reach for my bag. It isn't there. Of course. We'd left school without anything other than ourselves. 'Bonnie, do you have anything to eat on you?' Not that it will help if I don't have insulin.

She has to breathe into my ear for me to hear her. 'No. Nothing.' She pauses. 'Are you okay?'

'I'll be fine,' I say and realize that Bonnie doesn't understand code.

Neither of us has a watch. Neither of us has a phone. The sky doesn't let us guess the time. The aches in our muscles give us some idea that hours are passing. So does the ache in my stomach, the one bordering on pain. And the fuzziness I'm feeling in my head.

Another piece of roof gets whipped away and I can see the angry sky through the ever-increasing hole. How much rain can clouds hold? Cold creeps into my wet legs. I'm so, so tired but I have to get up and pee. I stand at the doorway and piss into the rain. It disappears into the wet air. I sit back down.

Finally, the storm eases. We can tell by the way the walls stop running and start dripping. The wind doesn't let up. In the distance, I hear another crash – and something else, a loud constant noise a bit like an aeroplane.

Bonnie lifts her head. 'That was intense.'

She is sitting close to me. Her head comes up under my chin and her hands are bunched at my stomach as I curl over her. I suddenly feel the movement of her back as she breathes and spread my fingers out over her school dress to feel it more. Despite the wet earth stink, I can smell her warm hair, her scalp, the washing detergent seeped into the collar of her dress. The storm, the rain, is gone for me. I have Bonnie in my arms. It's so magical that it almost takes everything else away. Almost.

We don't move until the wind stops yowling. By then the sky is dusky - I can tell even through the cloud cover. Bonnie straightens and I have to shift. We stand up, stretching. Mud falls off our feet in clumps. Bonnie reaches up and pushes her hair behind her ears. 'Should we go and see what happened?'

I follow her out.

It is hard to see in the near-dark but we push our way through wet saplings to the track and start down the hill. The road is covered in debris. I step over the branches I see, trip over the ones I don't. As we walk the plane-noise gets louder until it is in front of us. It is the creek, now a roaring river with its edges lapping at our feet.

'Oh my God,' says Bonnie. 'Look how wide it is!'

This is nothing like the creek watch in the worst of the times I've seen it. This is more like the flooding you get in tropical areas, in far-off Asian countries, in places I've never been to but watched on the TV. I can't quite see across but know from where I'm standing that the water has crept way up this side of the track and so must be at least that far up on the other side. The water churns dully, sticks and leaves racing madly and helplessly along it. They disappear into shadow.

'I don't think we can get across.'

Bonnie steps forward knee-deep into the water. 'Let's see.'

She's barely in before I see her fling her hands up as she's knocked off balance by the end of a racing branch. She wavers, I pounce on her, and we both end up sitting in the water. The strength and rush of it is frightening. Bonnie turns onto her hands and knees and staggers out. I'm a bit slower and cop another branch that whacks me neatly on the head as it goes past. I get out backwards like a crab, my head stinging.

Bonnie is on her feet and I struggle up as well. We look at each other in the musty darkness. 'You're bleeding,' she says loudly.

I brush my hair with my hand and it comes over streaked with something dark. 'We could try again.'

Bonnie shakes her head. 'There might be another way to get home.'

I look around us, but I'm no use because it's all unfamiliar territory to me. 'Do you know of any?'

'No.' She stares at the angry water. 'The creek is blocking the way back to town. Maybe we can't go anywhere until the water goes down.' She looks around. 'There are so many bush tracks we could follow but I don't know where any of them lead.'

The water is rising. I glance down at my feet and see it up around the heels of my shoes. Bonnie feels it, too. She leaps back as it washes over her socks. 'Maybe we could follow the water downstream,' I say. 'That will get us somewhere.'

The edge of the creek is now among the trees and shrubs of the bush. I leave the track and walk along it for a few metres. I'm feeling sicker and it's hard going. Trees block my way, shrubs slap me in the face. I can see less and less as the darkness really takes hold. I put my arms out in front of me like I imagine a blind man would walk, but still stumble over the ground and still get hit by water-laden branches.

'I don't think this is a good idea,' I yell back to Bonnie. 'I can't see where I'm going.' I stagger back to her, eyes on her brightest part – that white school dress collar - and she's standing in the water, eyes on me and not noticing anything else. Is it possible that the creek has risen even more?

Thunder and rain starts again.

I breathe slowly and calmly but there's a headache thumping at my forehead, warning me, telling me. I close my eyes and do some medical reasoning in my head. If I don't get any insulin soon, glucose won't be able to get into my blood and my body will start to break down. I think it might already be doing it. As if confirming my worst diagnoses, the sickness rises in me. I vomit into the scrub.

'Lewis?' Bonnie is there. I take her hand. 'I think we should wait in the hut for a while.'

We start back up the track, falling into the potholes under our feet, getting soaked more by this new rain. It takes us a while to find the hut again. We stagger up and down the track a few times until Bonnie finally recognizes a tall tree that leans out over the path. We turn into the bush. The old hut is a solid black against the shadowy darkness of the near-night. We push our way back in but it's not much of a shelter. Bonnie goes out and drags back two more fallen branches to put our feet on so at least we're out of the mud. The hut has a heavy rotten smell that it didn't have before. Nausea rolls around me and I swallow hard.

'It's getting cold,' says Bonnie so I wrap my arms around her. I don't think the temperature is that cold but we're wet and the wind cools us down. My body has been completely taken over by fuzz and seems slow to feel anything but after a while my teeth start to chatter. Bonnie wriggles out of my grip to put her arms around me.

The night falls black with no moon. We sit and wait, wait and sit. I get up to pee. The creek roars at us. Bonnie's voice goes distant. I faze in and out. Another tree comes down somewhere close with a terrifying crash that echoes around my head for ages. I keep my eyes closed and hope we stay alright.

37

BULL

'It's twelve o'clock midnight and here is the news...'

I stumble into my room and find a watch to confirm that the radio is right. So many hours have gone by. I stare into the blackness out the window and at last I see the glow of headlights and the glare of searchlights as an SES truck goes slowly past. It sets up a ripple of waves that reflect red and yellow, letting me see that the road is still covered with water but not as bad as it was. I don't think our old cars would handle it though. I go outside and stand on the veranda to watch as more trucks come and go.

A light pins me. Someone calls to me, 'You okay, mate?'

'Yeah, good.' I put my hand up to show how confident I am with this answer.

They move on in search of trouble and the light stabs other things.

At midnight, the reception on my phone creeps back. I ring Dad. He answers in two rings. 'Will? You alright?'

I feel strange when I hear his voice strangled with concern. I swallow before answering. 'I'm okay. The house is pretty wet, the ceiling's come down in the lounge-'

'But you're okay?'

Dad doesn't give a rats about the house, doesn't even hear that it's ruined. I smile. 'Yeah,' I say again. 'I'm good.'

'Listen, mate, I'm on the corner of High and Dunstan Streets and they'll let me through when the water goes down a bit. I'll be straight home then.'

'Okay, Dad. Where's Mum?'

'She's got the girls at the town hall. That's where they sent everyone when the water rose. They're fine.'

I promise to ring him if I need to then hang up. The street in front of me is getting busy as people venture out of their houses to check out the mess, but I stay where I am. The buckets still need to be changed. I text Lewis. *Crazy flood.* Then I remember that he thinks I'm crazy, not the weather. I text him again. *Crazier than me.* I keep working on the water-soaked house, not tired at all.

At five minutes to three o'clock there's a flash of head-lights in the driveway and Dad's car swings through the waterlogged gutter. He crashes out the door and I stand at the veranda post waiting. His hug is wrestler-like, his laugh long and relieved. For a while he just grips me then he starts rubbing my head. My eyes water and I have to say, 'Hey, Dad. Ouch.'

'Sorry, boyo.' He pushes me back to look at me and can't stop smiling. 'Bit wet inside?' He tips his head towards the house.

'Yeah.'

'Ah well,' he says, putting an arm around my shoulder and looking out to the street. 'Shit happens.' He eyeballs me. 'Don't tell your mother I said that.'

I shake my head.

We stand there for a while and watch the neighbourhood as more people arrive home. The emergency trucks roll through again followed by a silent police car with flashing lights. I hear our next door neighbours, Dawn and Johnno, discover that their bed has a collapsed and soggy ceiling on it. They are calling out so loudly to each other that Dad yells across the fence, 'At least you weren't in it.' I dunno that those wise words had much of an effect. Dawn starts sobbing.

At about half past three, Mum's car creeps along the road to park beside Dad's. Sofie jumps out first and rushes at him. Ella exits more gingerly, picking her way through the shallower puddles until she reaches me. 'You alright, Will?'

I nod.

She gives my arm a hug.

Mum is last. Her hands are glued together as she registers the damage to our street. I wait for her to burst past and into the house but she stops with the rest of us. Dad grabs her as she hesitates and pulls her towards him, his other arm still around Sofie. 'It's okay,' he says. 'See? Here we are.'

At first Mum doesn't do anything but slowly she lifts a hand to Dad's. She sees me watching her. 'Hello, William.'

'Hi Mum.'

She smiles, ghostly, and at last comes over to me. Her arms barely get around my middle and mine overlap on her back but the hug feels good.

'So, Will,' Dad says, 'on a scale of one to ten when one is not bad and ten is catastrophic, how's the house?'

I think carefully before answering. 'Six.'

It's a good answer for Dad, not so good for Mum. She squeezes her eyes closed for a few seconds and then snaps them open. There's a glint of resignation there. 'Let's go look then,' she says.

Before we can, the police car comes back and an officer gets out of his car. 'Initial check,' he says. I see that his pants are wet up past his knees. 'Damage?'

'Haven't been in yet,' says Dad.

'Ceilings and floors,' I say.

'Missing persons?'

'We're all here.'

'That's the main thing.' The police officer slams his book closed. 'You go and check your house.' He looks at Sofie. 'Keep the young ones away from wet areas until you know it's safe.' He wades back out to his car and drives next door to see Dawn and Johnno.

'What does he mean, Dad?' says Sofie.

'Well, we have to check that nothing is going to fall on us inside,' starts Dad.

'No. What's a missing person?'

'He's just checking that people's families are alright,' says Mum. 'We got separated from William, didn't we?'

'You cried,' Sofie says matter-of-factly.

I look at Mum and she shrugs at me. 'I was a bit worried.'

'No need,' says Dad, ever the happy guy. 'Will's good as gold.'

'Yeah,' I say a bit shakily thinking of Mum and Sofie and El at the Town Hall waiting out the hours in the storm. 'All good.'

Finally we go inside. El and I keep Sofie in the kitchen while Mum and Dad do an inspection with torches. I hear small cries from Mum and reassuring rumbles from Dad. From where we are, I can see the lounge room ceiling. Water is still dribbling from the hole but most of it is falling into the bin.

'Wait here,' I tell the girls and go to swap the bin and the saucepan over, bringing the bin back to empty in the sink. As I carry it back, Mum is standing at the couch. 'You set up all those buckets?'

I nod. 'I got a few of Dad's jumpers soaked.'

Dad comes in behind Mum and chuckles. 'Good work, kid. Great work.'

I'm watching Mum though, waiting for some sort of outburst about ruining Dad's clothes and using kitchen things for the wrong purpose, but instead she smiles. Just a small one but it bends her lips up in a friendly way. 'Yes. Good work, William.'

'Is it safe?' yells Sofie. Ella has her by the arm. 'Can I go into my bedroom?'

Dad decides that we can stay the rest of the night and work out what to do in the morning. It turns out that Sofie's room was the least affected so we all bunk down in there. Mum and Sofie fit on her tiny single bed. Ella and I lie on the floor. After a minute, after he tries to fit in like a wrongly shaped piece of jigsaw puzzle and fails, Dad takes his blanket out and lies in the corridor. In the shadows made by the line of slow moving vehicles outside, he looks a bit like a faithful guard dog keeping watch on his owners. Except that I think guard dogs wouldn't usually snore, and Dad does. Loudly.

I can't sleep. The night has been as long as a month but I still don't seem to be tired. I hear Sofie sleeping, her gentle night noises reminding me of when she was a baby and we used to watch her – Mum and Dad and Ella and me – just to see her soft, sleeping face. I can't hear Mum at all so think she's asleep.

Ella isn't. 'Will,' she says.

'Yeah?'

'What was it like? In the house with the storm?'

I think. 'Dark. Noisy.' I think more. 'Wet.'

'Were you scared?'

'A bit.'

There's quiet. Then, 'It was weird. At the hall. So many people were freaking out.'

'Why?'

'The power went out and the little kids were scared. Lightning hit the tree in the park – but I didn't see that. Then the hall leaked. There was water everywhere.'

'Were you scared?'

She thinks for a bit. 'No. Not until Mum started crying.'

'When did she do that?'

'When Dad came in and he didn't have you with him.'

'I was okay.'

There is a long silence and I think she's gone to sleep. 'Mum didn't think you were.'

'It's not like it was Cyclone Tracy.'

'Mum wasn't worried about the weather. She just thought-' she stops.

'What?'

'She thought *you'd* be freaked out. Because-' She stops again.

'What, Ella?'

'Because you've been so sad.'

I stare up at Sofie's fan. Its blades are darker than the ceiling so I can just make them out. It's weird that they're still because I always have my fan on. It's weird, too, that I'm trying to go to sleep on the floor with my sisters and mother in the room with me. Dad gives an extra loud snore as if to remind me that he's here as well. For the twentieth time, I say, 'I'm okay.'

'Are you really?' El seems to be holding her breath.

'I think so. For now, anyway.'

We stop talking and I finally drift into sleep. As I fade away, I hear Mum for the first time. She's sighing, a deep long heavy breath out, and I know that she's heard every word we just said.

———

IT RAINS AGAIN the next day but it's nothing like the day before. We stay home because school is closed, and spend a few hours mopping water away. Dad pulls the carpet up where it's wet and separates it from its underlay. The house stinks so Mum opens all doors and windows. The rain is gentle but constant so we can't hang anything out. Dad checks the ceiling and uses a thick piece of plastic to patch the roof leak that caused the most trouble. The dribbles stop. Mum towels the walls dry.

The power comes back on. Straight away, Dad hooks up a heater and the house fills with wet dog stink from the drying carpet. Mum starts the washing machine. The sounds of a normal if busy home fill the place. She cooks us a chocolate cake and we eat it warm standing at the kitchen bench, ignoring the humidity that makes us sweat as we munch.

Afterwards, I go over to the hole in the lounge ceiling and study it. Dad has done a good job getting rid of the soggiest bits of plaster but it did make the hole bigger. He comes to have a look. 'Well,' he says. 'Don't know if I did the right thing there.'

I shrug.

We look a bit longer then Dad turns to pat the top of the piano. 'You got it all the way out here by yourself?'

The piano is sitting in the centre of the room. The wet in the carpet didn't reach it. I stroke some cobwebs from its back. 'Yep.'

Dad does a hair-ruffle and I wince. 'You did a nice job of handling things, being here all by yourself, Will.'

I think of the way the water came through the plaster and what it would have done if it had hit the piano. 'I didn't really have a choice.'

'All the same. Things would have been worse if you didn't act the way you did.'

The phone rings, startling us. I hadn't realized it was back on. Dad's the first to get to it. 'Hopefully an insurance inspector,' he says wryly as he picks it up. 'Hello?'

His eyes go to me. It's not the insurance inspector.

'No, no, he's not here.' Pause. 'Hang on.' He holds the phone out to me. 'Will.'

'Hello?'

The Judge's brisk voice is on the other end. 'I'm looking for Lewis, William. Would you know where he is?'

Lewis. I remember his angry eyes and the spit of his voice. I remember that I was just the same. 'No. I haven't seen him for days.'

'Did he say anything to you then that I should know about?'

This confuses me. Should I tell her that Lewis thinks I've gone mad? Is that what she's asking? I try to think past our last conversation. 'Lewis was feeling great. He said he wasn't sick anymore.'

That must have meant something to her because I hear her breathing at the end of the phone but not saying anything.

'Mrs Pascoe?'

She speaks again, her voice a bit distant as if she's holding the phone away from her mouth. 'I haven't seen Lewis since yesterday morning. Charles Gates said that he saw him at school at lunchtime. Mark Kendon said the same. No one remembers seeing him after then. That was before the storm.'

'Have you talked to Grace or Jules or Bonnie?' I say. 'They might know.'

'No. Thank you. I will.' She puts the phone down.

'Everything alright?' asks Dad.

'Lewis is missing,' I say and the words sink into me like a slow burn. 'His mum can't find him.'

'Ah.' Dad rubs his forehead. 'He'll turn up.'

I'm not convinced by Dad's words. He isn't either because he turns away from me but keeps rubbing his head. I put the phone on the bench and look out into the weather. So much rain, I wouldn't have thought it possible to have so much rain in one day. 'What do you think it's like at the creek watch, Dad?'

Dad is standing under the hole again, gazing up as if it had all the answers. 'I heard that you can't get anywhere near the creek or the watch. The water's over the bridge.'

I think of the deep running creek and how the road crosses it. It must be like a river. No cat would survive the creek now. The thought makes me go to my bedroom and seek out my phone. There's one message on it but it isn't Lew. It's Kendo and it was sent yesterday. *WHAT ABOUT THIS CRAZY STORM???* I can hear the blood pumping through him into the phone. I delete it, stuff the phone into my pocket, and wander out to Dad.

'What do we do now, Dad?'

He looks at me, his face a readable mix of worry and tiredness. 'We wait, mate. That's what we do right now.'

I stare up at the hole but it hasn't got any other answers for me either.

38

BULL

'I'm going out to help Andrew. His roof needs covering.' Dad gets his toolkit from the shed and waves to us once before he goes.

The water is gone from the street. I watch him drive carefully along the asphalt. As he leaves, the sun breaks through the cloud and makes the wet roads glisten. Dad slows down even more. I imagine the glare blinding him.

'That's about all I can do for now,' says Mum to no one in particular. Ella's sitting in the kitchen drinking Milo. Sofie's tucked away in her room.

I turn around, restless and nervy. 'I'm going for a walk, Mum.'

'Stay away from any running water,' she says automatically before looking at me straight. 'Where are you going?'

'Just round the block. See what damage's been done.'

'I'm coming with you.' Ella slips off her stool and pokes her feet into her sneakers.

We leave before Mum can give us too many mother-lectures about being careful. The gutters are still running, thick with slush. I look around for Lewis as if he might be hiding behind a tree or a fence to jump out and scare me.

As we walk around the corner and down the hill, the water runs along the footpath next to us. The gutter water here is wide and wild. Sticks and rubbish litter it. The further we go, the wider the water gets until by the time we reach the corner, a whole dam of water blocks the road. A small group of people stand watching the whirling mess. A man in shorts is poking at the storm water drain with a long stick but it doesn't seem to be helping the water escape.

We skirt around the edge and make our way along the path, walking hard up against the brick fences of the houses to keep our feet dry. Ella stops suddenly outside her friend Molly's house. 'Look.' She points but it's obvious. A tree has come down and smashed the garage. There's no sign of anyone home. Tree roots face the road, a dark mass of mud and ripped ends. It's such a strange sight that we keep going. I try not to look and Ella can't help but look.

Further up the street we see flooded cars parked along the road, a thick tree branch speared into a roof, and a collapsed brick wall of a half-built house. Maybe Lewis is caught in storm wreckage? I start looking more closely but see nothing that resembles a skinny sixteen year old boy trapped anywhere. A bad feeling is curling in my stomach. The damage around us is reinforcing it. Where are you, Lewis? Why haven't you come home?

A woman is standing next to a small hatchback. Water gushes around her calves as she struggles to open the car door. She hasn't got the strength and I wonder why she's trying when I see a little white dog face appear at the windscreen. The dog is trapped in the car and the woman can't get to it. I see her getting more frantic as she tugs at the door. The water pushes back, not letting her in.

'Will,' says Ella, pointing at the dog.

'Yeah, I see. Hang on.'

Ella waits on the footpath as I step out onto the road. The woman turns towards me, her face twisted in sadness. I stop. It's the Bitch Lady. Michelle, the one who makes my life Hell.

'Please. Can you help?'

She's so upset that she doesn't see who I am. I think about leaving her but what has that dog – the one in the car – ever done to hurt me? I hear Ella give a little yell as the dog does a circle of the interior of the car and comes back to look at us through the glass. For the dog's sake, I wade into the water. Michelle steps aside. I wrench at the car door. It takes three or four pulls but the door creaks open, gets caught in the water, and snaps out all the way. It hits Michelle in the knees and she gasps. The dog bounds across the seats, ready to leap out into the street. I catch it as it does because it would have hit the water and been gone down the gutter and into the drain.

The little white thing struggles hard to be free but I've got big arms. I go backwards out of the water and Michelle follows, her eyes on the dog, a big smile on her face that shows all her lumpy teeth.

I hand it over.

'Thanks,' she says. 'Thanks so much. I just couldn't do it. Thank God you came along.'

I wait for her to recognise me but she doesn't. I think about saying something but realise I don't have to. She'll know me when I go back to work. She'll just have to see me that one time and she'll remember what I've done. I nod and turn away from her, knowing I won't worry anymore. She's got nothing more that she can say to me. I go back to Ella who pats my arm in appreciation of my fantastic rescue mission. We walk off with the sounds of a happy yapping dog behind us.

THE NEXT CORNER is free of water so we turn up the hill again. There are signs of life along here as people start to carry bits of wet furniture into the sun to speed up the drying process. I count three armchairs, six mattresses and a heap of pillows. I also see four dead magpies and one lost cat that won't come near us even when Ella calls to it.

The last corner leads us back to our place. We might be downhill from the pool but we aren't at the very bottom and I can see now how lucky it was that we weren't. Our house seems to have escaped the worst of the flood damage. As we get to the front of it, there's Mum hanging rugs on the veranda rail to catch the strengthening sun. 'I better go and help,' says Ella quietly.

'I'm going to walk up further,' I say.

I start in the direction that Dad went, suddenly hanging out to ask him again what to do. I've waited and nothing's happened. What's next? Kids are riding their bikes in the street now, swishing in and out of the gutters like heroes. The clouds break up even further. The sun is making the roads steam and I'm wet through from the humidity. I'm just thinking that maybe Dad drove further than I thought he did when the ambulance whizzes past and stops in front of a white weatherboard house. I look more closely. Dad's car is parked there, as well.

Stuff the heat. I run, as fast as my bulk will let me. I get to the house to see three ambos kneeling on the ground beside a body even bigger than mine. From the corner of my eye, a blue tarp flaps lazily with a gentle breeze, but I'm staring at Dad lying on the ground groaning quietly.

'Dad!' I crash towards him but am held back by a guy I vaguely know as Dad's mate. 'Easy, Will. It's okay – he slid off the roof. I think it's his collar bone.'

An ambulance officer glances up at me. For a startling second, I think it might be the guy that took Josh away, the man from the club, but it isn't. Neither are the other ambos. I feel so relieved at that, it's stupid. It doesn't mean that Dad isn't seriously injured just because Josh was dead when the other ambulance officer turned up. This one says to me, 'You his son? Come around and talk to him.'

I pull away and go to Dad's side. He looks at me and does the best smile he can. 'Hey, buddy. They don't make ladders like they used to.'

'We'll take him in for investigation,' says someone official. 'Can you let your mum know?'

'I'm ringing now,' says Dad's friend, holding his phone up.

'Can I come with you?' I say to Dad and he looks up at the guy with the trolley who shakes his head. 'No, mate. You can come in with your mum.'

'William, you stay with the girls, okay? Let Mum come in by herself.'

They load him onto the trolley and it creaks under his weight. Now that he's sucking on a green whistle, the white pain has lifted from his face and his grin is sloppy. I wave goodbye and head back home where Mum is already in the car. 'I'll be back as soon as I can be,' she says grimly.

'We'll be fine.'

She drives away through the sluice.

Because I saw Dad, I'm not as worried as I see Ella is. Kendo broke his collar bone at school playing footy a couple of years ago. He walked into the ambulance with his arm in a sling and his head muddy from the face plant he'd done on the field. One of Kendo's party tricks is to show us the bump where the bone ends knitted back together. But Ella's never seen anyone with a broken collar bone. She chews her lip for a while until she puts on *Toy Story* for Sofie and then they sit down to wait.

More waiting, just when I'd decided that I couldn't do it anymore. I pull my phone from my pocket and check for texts even though I know there aren't any because I would have felt vibes if anyone had sent one. *Dad's in hospital* I send to Lewis because even if he's angry at me, he'll want to know how Dad is. I leave the phone on the bench but nothing happens. I take the land line and ring The Judge.

The phone is answered half way through the second ring. 'Lewis?'

My heart does a downhill leap. 'No, it's William. I was just ringing to see whether Lewis…'

'No. We haven't found him yet.' The Judge pauses and I hear low conversation in the background. 'I rang Bonnie Valentine's house but there's no answer. They may have evacuated because of the storm.'

I think of the tree on Molly's house. I remember where Bonnie lives and think that it luckily doesn't have many big trees.

'Did he leave a note?' I ask.

'No. And no-one saw him after lunch. Will, I'm sorry, but I have to go. We want to keep the phone free. You know, just in case.'

I understand. I nod, realize she can't see, and say, 'I'll go now.'

'We'll ring you when we find him.'

The dead phone is loud in my ear but I hold it there while I think. Lewis has never dodged out of school, I'm sure of that because if he'd done it in the past I would have gone with him. Why hadn't Charlie and Kendo seen him after lunch? What if he'd forgotten something and gone back home to get it but the storm had caught him and now he was stranded somewhere surrounded by water? Maybe he didn't go home but where else would he have gone? Especially without me?

I put the phone back. I'm not sure what to do and wish like crazy that Dad was here to help or that I'd least had a chance to talk to him before he fell off the roof. I feel guilty thinking that. Dad will be in pain. He hates doctors and he'll be surrounded by them. He didn't have the accident on purpose to avoid my questions. I should have asked Lewis's mum where they've looked for him but the police aren't stupid, they would have looked everywhere they can think. Where would he have gone that the police wouldn't know about?

I can't hang around here any longer. 'Ella,' I say. 'I'm going out for a bit.'

'You can't, Will.' she says, almost tearfully. 'What about Dad?'

'It's just his collar bone.'

'You don't know that for sure,' Ella says angrily.

She's right but I've got other things on my mind and I can't let the thought of Dad being more injured than I realize stop me from looking for Lewis. 'I'll have my phone on me and I'm not going far.' It's not as if I can drive. I try the Big Brother act. 'Are you okay with Sofie?'

Sofie sticks her head over the back of the couch. 'I'll look after Ella.'

I smile at her. She could try. Not very successfully, I wouldn't think. 'I'll be back in one hour, El. Tops.'

Ella watches me as I go, giving me daggers with her eyes. I shut the door, squint against the glare of the sun, and start walking up the hill to the pool. Hey, it's where we always meet. Maybe Lewis will be there.

The town looks like a disaster zone. There's hardly a

house around that hasn't got something drying in the sun. The water has gone from the hill but it has left its mark by a line of muck on the road and fences. It's steaming hot in the sun. It seems to be working overtime and trying to make everything better again by heating up the world. A rim of black soulless clouds sit on the horizon, threatening more bad weather. The sun, I think, is trying to burn them away.

My phone is in my hand as I walk. I go past Kendo's turn off and think about ringing him but my legs walk on past before my head can make up its mind. I trudge the rest of the way to the pool where the car park is full of fire trucks and police cars. There's a group of kids watching.

'What's going on?' I ask the tallest one who I think I recognize from school.

'Dunno,' he says. 'Something's happened at the pool.'

The fire trucks are fanned out around the pool entrance. I can't see any smoke and can't believe it would be a fire in this weather anyway. 'Maybe they're just using the car park as a meeting place.'

The tall kid just shakes his head. Yeah, he's right. They wouldn't be parked like they are if they were just meeting. We stand around for maybe ten minutes and watch fire officers dressed in overalls walk briskly to and fro, talking into two way radios. A couple go through the pool entrance and don't come back out. Minutes later, an ambulance arrives. We move out of the way but it isn't in a hurry. It pulls up next to the trucks and when they get out I see that they're the same blokes that got Dad off the ground. They don't look at me, though. They go through the gate.

This time the wait is only a minute. One of the little kids comes haring back on his bike, important news dripping off him like sweat. 'There's a body in the pool,' he says even before he's stopped. We jump out of his way and he brakes so sharply that the bike skids. 'Floating up the deep end.'

'You saw it?' says someone.

'Yeah. Well, almost. They haven't got it out yet.'

A body? I'm suddenly cold in the bright hot white glaring sunshine. I think it's Lewis. I know it's him. I almost die on the spot. He can't be dead if the last time I spoke to him I hated his guts. That wouldn't be fair, that wouldn't be fair at all.

Is it possible to have a nightmare while you're awake? One minute, ordinary things are happening and then the monsters creep in. You're not aware of them straight away but their blackness starts to colour your day. The sky, which you had thought was blue, darkens and the fear rises in your throat. Even though you know it's only a nightmare, it doesn't make it any better.

Sometimes my memory plays tricks and I think I remember things happening that actually didn't. Like the day Josh left. I know it was hot. It was red. But *what* was red? His body? My body? Did I hold him until the ambulance came? I can't remember the details, only the colour red.

I have a few nightmares that keep coming back to me and I'm not sure whether they are re-enactments of things I've seen or just twisted versions of the real thing. They come at night, though, not during the day. No one's ever heard of daymares.

Lewis is in the pool. This is a daymare.

39

BULL

I run up to the entrance but am blocked by a strong fireman. 'Let go,' I say. 'Lewis is in there.'

'Hang on a minute,' the man says, gripping my arms tightly. 'No one can go in.'

'But it's Lewis. He's missing.' I struggle, he grips painfully tight.

'You can't go in. You have to go home.'

A police officer joins him and they exchange glances. I don't care if they think I'm crazy.

'I have to go and check whether it's Lewis!'

There's a group of people at the pool edge – police, fireman and the two ambos. They have a stretcher with something on it. Some*one* on it. Lewis on it.

'It's Lewis,' I say again.

The fireman turns me away and marches me down the hill. I'm big but he's stronger. I have no choice but to go with him. 'Listen, mate,' he says gently. 'I can't let you go in and I can't let you know who that is in there. Is Lewis your brother?'

'He's my friend.' I suddenly realize how pathetic that sounds. 'He's my best friend.'

The fireman nods. The police officer joins us again. She notices the other kids watching. 'Hey,' she says, 'you kids get going. There's nothing you want to see here.'

'Dunno about that,' mutters the tall kid but as the fireman starts walking towards them, they turn and leave.

In that short time, the ambos have brought the body out on a trolley. I twist around but the fireman is still holding me firmly. The body is covered in a sheet and it's hard to see its size. Is it as tall as Lewis? Is it as skinny? I can't see properly because of the crowd of uniforms around it. They load it into the ambulance and shut the door.

'My friend is missing,' I say to the police officer this time. 'I just need to know who you've got.' My voice is shaking and sounds weird. 'Please.'

The police officer and the fireman look at each other. 'We can't say, I'm sorry,' the police officer says. She looks sad. 'You need to go home now.'

'I can't,' I say. It's true. I seem to be stuck here. 'Lewis is sixteen, tall and skinny. You could at least tell me if it *isn't* him.'

'What's your name?' The police officer signals to the fireman and he lets me go but doesn't move away.

'Will,' I say. 'William Healey.'

'Will, we can't give you any identity on who we found. It wouldn't be fair on the relatives of the deceased. What about I give you a ride home?' She smiles at me, a nice smile but not one I want.

'Lewis has been missing since yesterday.' My eyes are suddenly filling with tears. 'That's too long.'

'We've had reports of twelve people missing since the storm, Will. We're looking for everyone as fast as we can.

Come on.' She puts her arm out as if to wave me towards the police car. I look over at the ambulance. It's ready to drive away.

'Can I at least go and look at the pool? I might notice something that you didn't.'

The police officer looks at the fireman and shrugs. 'Alright then, but only if I take you in.'

The ambulance leaves with the unidentified someone in the back. I don't run after it although my body pulls towards it. I follow the police officer through the pool entrance.

The pool is a mess. The shade sails have been ripped from their poles. Leaves and branches stain the blue water. The plastic climb-on mushroom in the kids' pool has been flattened by a piece of torn-away roof iron. I get the feeling that people left the pool area in a hurry, maybe only just before the storm, because towels and bags are caught on fences and wrapped around the poles. I stumble over a bright pink pair of kids' sandals.

If Lewis had been here, I think in the logical part of my head, then someone would have seen him. Charlie or Kendo or Jules or Grace or Bonnie or someone who's wagging because it's a hot day. Someone from school is always at the pool if it's a hot enough day. 'Do you know if he was seen here yesterday?' I ask the police officer.

She shakes her head. 'I don't know the story behind your friend going missing. We have too many people to account for.'

I look around for Lewis's stuff. School bag, maybe. Faded green beach towel that seems to be the only one he has. The illogical side of my brain is saying that he might have come here after everyone else had evacuated. Maybe he was so hot that he ignored the storm warnings and crept in through the gate when the lifeguards weren't looking.

I don't see any sign of anything that belongs to him even after I turn over every piece of shit in the place. The police officer stands back and watches me, talking into her radio every now and then. When finally I stand lost in the middle of the ruined grass, she walks down to me. 'Come on, mate. I'll run you home.'

'Nothing,' I say. 'Then it couldn't be him. Could it?' I feel calmer, my heart rate has slowed.

She only looks at me sympathetically. Police officers must be trained in the art of being neutral. 'Come on,' she says again.

She gives me a ride down the hill to home and waves once as I leave the car in silence. Inside, Ella is sitting on the arm of the couch biting her fingernails and Sofie is drawing a picture of Buzz. El looks up as I come in. I must look pretty terrible because she sits up straight and says, 'What's wrong?'

'Someone drowned in the pool.'

'Yuck,' says Sofie.

'Who?' says Ella.

'I don't know. They wouldn't say.' I look towards the phone. 'Any news?'

'No.' El slumps again, goes back to her nails.

I can't stand the silent phone so I go into my bedroom and shut the door. My guitar is a shadow in the corner. My bedside table is dusty where my base station had sat. I wonder for a second whether I'm in the right room then I see the tangled, sweaty, stinking sheets on my bed, disgusting after all those hours I spent in them.

They make me feel sick and I pull them off the bed, flinging Josh's notebook out at the same time. It flies across the room and lands against the wardrobe door with a thump, cracking open at the blank page where I'd taken off the photo of Len. I stand and stare at it, thinking of how Josh's story was in it for us to read when he was dead.

What if you're already doing it?

Lewis's words appear like a neon billboard in my brain. While Josh's notebook is finished and mine never started, Lewis had said that his was already here. The story of Lewis, right up to this point in time. The history of Lewis.

I bolt out of my room. 'Ella,' I yell, 'I'm going to Lewis's.'

'No you aren't,' she screams back. 'You have to wait here with us!'

'I can't.'

'Will! Dad's in hospital. We haven't heard anything. You can't leave us again!'

I pause in my frenzy and see her pale frightened face. 'Dad'll be okay. He's just broken his collar bone.'

'How do you know that? He fell off a *roof*, Will. He could have all sorts of injuries. Maybe that's why it's taking so long!'

I clamp my jaws together. I *don't* know why Mum hasn't rung and let us know what's going on. I think of the ambulance delivering that dead body to the hospital. 'They'll be busy at the hospital, Ella. Dad's probably waiting in a queue. Worse things could have happened to other people.'

'How do we know that it isn't worse?' Ella looks at me as if my brain is custard. 'Stop being such an arsehole, Will.'

I bite my lip, trying not to think of Dad bleeding to death from internal injuries. I remember his face as he was being loaded into the ambulance. He didn't look like he was badly injured, he looked like he was pretty high from those pain killers. I think back and forth and back. Dad is in hospital but Lewis is nowhere. There's nothing I can do for Dad at the moment but Lewis is another matter. The daymare flashes into my head so suddenly I jump. 'Ella, I really need to go to Lewis's. I've got my phone with me so you can ring if you need to.'

'Will…'

I don't often see tears from my sister so when they flow down her cheeks I feel bad. Then angry. All Ella has to do is to sit here and watch DVDs with Sofie. She'll be fine. I have to do something else. I shake my head at her. 'Ring me if you want me. I'll come straight home.'

I run out the door so I don't have to look at her face. The sun is blazing but I can feel the air thickening ready for more storms. The sun really doesn't have a chance. There are more people around as everyone comes outside for a sticky beak at our wrecked town. Everyone's too busy gazing at the water or the fallen branches to worry about me. I decide to go right around the hill to Lewis's. I can't face that pool again.

It strikes me, as I'm halfway there, that if the body in the pool is Lewis then I'll arrive at the house at about the same time as the police will get there. I mean, I've watched the crime shows on T.V. The police have a list of missing people. They'll match the body to the list. Then they'll go around to that person's house. The thought makes me slow down until I'm almost shuffling but I don't stop. I won't stop because sooner or later I'll have to know.

It takes me an age to reach the house. I pass a group of crying children as they stand looking at the remains of a cubby house in their front yard. Their mum is patting them and making those noises that mothers make to little kids when they're trying to make things better. 'There, there. It's all right. Never mind.' I can't remember when my mum last said that to me and I feel a bit jealous of those tiny kids. It'll stop one day, I want to say to them.

One day, you have to get over it yourself. I feel bitter at the thought.

'Bull!'

A figure looms out of a house and runs towards me.

'Charlie! You scared the shit out of me.'

'Yeah. You look like you're a million miles away.' He crosses his arms and we stare around the soggy landscape. 'Going to Lewis's?'

'Yeah.'

'Any news?'

'I'm going to see.'

'Okay.' He uncrosses his arms, crosses them again.

'Someone's drowned in the pool, Charlie.'

'God! Who?'

'I don't know. I don't...'

I see the same terrible thought cross his mind that is pelting through mine. He stares at me, open mouthed, until he can get some words out. 'Want me to come with you to Lewis's?'

Charlie has been a friend of mine since primary school. Not a really close friend, not one that I shared my deep dark secrets with when Josh died, but a background friend. He comes to my birthdays, I go to his. When it's school social time, he's one of the pack and he stands in the corner with Lewis and me and drinks his Coke while we watch Kendo dance with girls. Yeah, he's the sort of bloke who is always there. But I can't do this to him. I can't take the easy way out when the last time I spoke to Lew I was full of spite and anger. 'No, it's all right,' I say. 'His mum promised to ring if there was any news and she hasn't. So there can't be any news. Right?'

He lets his arms go once and for all. They hang limply. 'Right,' he says.

'I'll see you later.'

'Yeah.'

I walk on.

Another five minutes and I'm at Lewis's house. There's a bunch of cars outside but no sign of the police. The relief makes me dizzy so it's a while before I can go to the door and knock. Almost immediately, it's answered by some random who asks me – nicely – what I want. 'I'm Will,' I say. 'I'm a friend of Lewis's.'

'Right,' says the woman, who is a complete stranger to me. 'Well, come in, I suppose. Miranda is talking to the police.'

Miranda? I think. That's The Judge. Another thought arrives a split second later - police?

I follow the woman in to the kitchen and find The Judge and Mr Pascoe at the table with two other people I've never seen before. Plain clothes cops. My heart rate rises. Of course. Plain clothes, plain car.

Lewis's mum doesn't even look at me. Mr P stares out the window, turns to catch my eye and gives me a quick nod. I stare at the police, two men with intense faces. I'm finding it a bit hard to tune in to what they're saying, but I catch some words. 'Keep looking. Other areas. No clues.'

I breathe out, slow and long. *Keep looking.* That means they haven't found him. That means it wasn't him in the pool! That means he's still out there somewhere.

I hear my words before I can remember thinking them. 'I might have a clue.'

The adults turn to me like I'm holding a lottery prize ticket.

The Judge - Miranda - lets me into Lewis's room and I look around for his notebook. The police stand in the hall at a respectful distance. The curtains are open, the window is up and a hot breeze floods the room. I see the notebook stacked on his desk with his other school books but when I pull it out and open it, there's nothing in it but that first newspaper article Mrs Mac had put in. Numbly, I read the headline. *Anti-climatologists say global warming is a joke.* I think of the storm we've just had and don't find anything funny about it.

'Did you find anything, William?' Lewis's mum is trying hard not to sound eager but as I turn to her, she knows. 'Oh.'

But then it dawns on me. 'No, hang on. I've got the wrong book.' I slam Mrs Mac's notebook shut and drop it on Lewis's bed. I'm hunting now for the sketchbook, that one that he bought at the art supply shop. Black. Spiral bound. Hard cover. It doesn't seem to be here. Maybe Lewis took it with him?

'Was there anything missing from here, Mrs Pascoe? Did Lewis take anything?'

'He didn't take a thing.' She nudges Lewis's school bag with one foot, and pats that blue bag of his with one hand. 'That's the worry. We found this at school. It means he doesn't have any medication with him.'

The problems with that are written all over her pale face. I feel sick. No matter what Lewis said about being well at the moment, he wouldn't stay that way without his insulin.

I can't see the sketchbook anywhere on the desk. I look under the bed, next to the mattress and through the pile of school books on the floor. I zip open his school bag and up-end its contents onto the carpet. Nothing. And then I notice the neat row of books along the shelf. The last one is a bit smaller than the rest and I remember how he'd bought a different one that day we were in the art shop. I reach up and take if off the shelf. 'This is what I was looking for.'

Lewis's mum snatches it away and flicks through it

frantically. The police peer in, but don't say anything. As The Judge nears the end, I can see her start shaking her head. 'No, no, no,' she says. She gets to the end and looks at me, the frantic-ness plastered on her face. 'What was meant to be in it, William?'

I'm not sure that I can explain so I hold out my hand for the book and she passes it over slowly. 'I thought it might give me some idea of where he is,' I say lamely.

'We've searched this room,' says one police officer. 'There don't seem to be any leads.' He backs away into the corridor, and Mr P takes them outside to have a final look in the backyard as if they might discover Lewis there asleep on a deck chair. I feel stupid, like I've made people believe in something that wasn't real and now I've hurt them. Badly.

The phone rings. Lewis's mum exits, fast. I hear the threads of the conversation ('No, Mum, there's no word…') and realize that him being missing has set up a ripple of worry that probably extends across the state if not the whole of the world. I sit down on his bed and start looking through the book.

The first thing I notice is the pictures of Bonnie. Lewis's *numerous* pictures of Bonnie. I feel a bit embarrassed. Bonnie? Out of all the girls that we know, Lewis focuses on Bonnie? And why hadn't I noticed? My embarrassment turns to shame. I see Bonnie's triumphant stance over Jordan and fidget a bit. I go back to the beginning of the book and look through it again.

This book is nearly entirely Bonnie. Lewis has drawn her mysterious, detailed, beautiful. I feel wrong looking at how carefully he's traced her face and hands. It's sort of like looking through naked pictures but Bonnie isn't really nude, I'm just feeling the way Lewis has drawn her. I knew he was good at art, I knew he could draw. But this…this is amazing. Each page takes me longer to look at but I reach the end of the sketchbook again and close it softly.

I haven't got any clues to where Lewis is but I've got a very clear picture of who he might be with.

I go out to The Judge but she's still on the phone. The police have gone for now. The Judge seems to have forgotten me and looks surprised as I go past. I have Lewis's sketchbook tucked under one arm. I think she sees that I have it. I take the chance that she has so I'm not technically stealing. Anyway, she turns away from me and rests her head on her phone-free hand. I figure she's got enough to think about without me giving her false hope again. What would I say? 'I think Lewis has a girlfriend'? Yeah, just what she wants to hear.

SOMETHING MAKES me notice how late it's getting. Cloud across the sun, maybe, playing tricks with the shadows. I pull out my phone to see what the time is. The screen is blank. It's flat. Great. I've left the girls at home, Ella still crying maybe, and I have a flat phone.

I shuffle home in the impression I do of a run. As I round the corner, splashing through the puddles that have gathered in a blocked gutter, I see Mum's car. I hear her voice even before I get in the door but it's okay, she's talking to Dad. One arm in a sling, a graze down the side of his face, but still looking a lot better than he could have. Except for the thunderous blackness of his face as he spots me.

'William,' he roars, 'we asked you to stay at home with your sisters.'

Dad doesn't often roar. He usually saves it for life-threatening conditions. I hope it's not my life he's threatening now. 'I'm sorry,' I say straight away. 'I went to Lewis's.'

Immediately Dad's face changes. 'They've found him?'

'No. I went to see if I could help.'

Dad's not quite sure what to do. I suspect that, despite the drugs they would've pumped into him at the hospital, his bones are hurting like shit. He shifts around uncomfortably and winces, then winces again as his wince pulls at the grazes on his face. 'I see.'

I look up at Mum but she seems to have had enough. She sits on a kitchen stool, looking defeated. I don't know why: is it Dad? Lewis? Me? I say the first thing that comes into my head. 'Someone drowned in the pool.'

'I know,' she says. 'We were at the hospital when the body came in.'

'Do you know who it was?'

'They wouldn't say. She was a local, that's all I know.'

'*She?*'

'Yes.' Mum stares at me and says softly, 'Did you think it was Lewis?'

I nod, shrug, shake my head. 'I was at the pool when they...' I hadn't even thought it might have been a girl. 'I went around to see his mum and dad. I thought that if it was, they'd already...'

Dad clears his throat, looking wretched. 'Do they need help, William? Searching or anything?'

'The police are there. I don't think so.' Somehow, tears have escaped my eyes and slide relentlessly down my cheeks. 'I thought that if I looked through his things, I might have noticed something.'

'And you didn't.' Dad leans his good arm on my shoulder. 'It's not your fault.'

A cold wind seems to blow across my skin. I remember him saying that before, those many months ago when Josh died before I could catch him. It's one of those statements that doesn't really mean anything because the words have no effect on the person they're aimed at. Someone either knows in their soul that they are at fault or they aren't. Doesn't matter what someone else says. This *is* my fault because if we hadn't have had that argument, if I hadn't have felt the need to take to my bed, then I would know why Lewis left school in the morning. I'd know where to find him now. Just like if I'd been able to run faster, I would have caught Josh before he took that plunge out of the tree. It may not have been all my fault that my cousin died, but I'm partly to blame.

How much am I to blame for Lewis?

40

BULL

'Dad's asleep, Mum.' Sofie is staring at Dad's arm wrapped in a sling and propped on one of Mum's frilly pillows.

'Let him sleep.'

Ella puts on another one of those girly DVDs. Mum finishes the kitchen clean-up and comes to sit in the lounge room as well. Her eyes are rimmed with tiredness. She glances over to where I perch on the piano stool but it's okay, I'm not going to wake Dad up. The piano is back where it should be but the lid is closed because I don't play anymore. I'm just sitting here because there's nowhere else to go.

My re-charged phone rings. Unknown number. 'Hello?' I say and hear the desperation in my voice. It startles me how hopeless I sound.

'Bull?'

I pause in disbelief. '*Grace?*'

There's silence while we think about each other at the ends of the line. At least, I think of Grace with her strong legs and her wild hair.

'You've been sick,' she says bluntly.

I think of those empty hours, the empty thoughts. Sick? I don't know what to say.

She doesn't wait long enough for an answer. 'No one can find Bonnie.' Her voice is strange.

Bonnie's missing? I think of the pool, the girl that drowned in the pool. 'Grace,' I say slowly, 'there was someone in the pool.'

'The woman from the video shop.'

'What?'

'It was the lady from the video shop. The one with the blonde hair.'

'How do you know?'

'Mum knows someone who works in the hospital. She told us.' There's a pause. 'I thought it might be Bonnie.'

We are silent for a moment. I'm thinking of the video shop without the blonde lady. I'm thinking of my life without Lewis.

'Bull?'

'I thought it was Lewis,' I break in. 'Before I knew it was a girl. Lewis is still missing.' I walk as I talk. I go into my room and shut the rest of my family out. 'They're looking all over the place.'

'I think Lewis and Bonnie are together.'

The sketchbook is on the bed beside me. I flick it open randomly but it's a picture of Bonnie. One of the many pictures of Bonnie. 'Yes.' Quiet falls again and then I hear Grace breathing as if she's squashing the phone to her face. The thought makes my heart race. 'Grace? I think you're right.'

'I know I'm right. They are together.' The firmness with which she says this gives me hope. Lewis on his own seems so much worse than Lewis with Bonnie.

'They could be trapped by the water,' I say.

We think about this, her best friend and my best friend marooned somewhere in the flood.

'Bull, I'm coming over to see you. I can't stand waiting around here doing nothing.'

My head whirls a bit. Grace at my place? I look around at my soulless room. 'If you want to.'

'Yeah, I do.'

I give her directions to my house even though I think that if Bonnie's mum knew how to get here, Grace will as well. Then I don't know what to do next. I go into the kitchen and stand in the dim light to wait. The television echoes canned laughter and from my vantage point I see that Mum has fallen asleep as well, her arm across her face as if to shield herself from the world. Ella and Sofie sit side by side on beanbags and Sofie flops her head across to El. I see Ella's arm wrap around Sofie's shoulders. They look so comfortable that I feel a twang of jealousy shoot through me.

It's not long before there's a knock at the door and Grace is standing there in the twilight. She's wearing her singlet top and shorts and her hair is zinging all over the place. I briefly wonder what I look like. Her eyes are wide. She looks different. I realize what it is. Grace is scared. Tough Grace of the Black Tattoos is scared.

I'm scared too. She sees it on my face as well. She holds my gaze for a moment before I step back and let her in.

We go into my room – with Ella's eyes following us – and for something to do, I show Grace the sketchbook with its endless pictures of Bonnie. She pauses for a long time at each drawing, going 'Ha!' as she sees the one of Bonnie standing over Jordan. When she finishes, she goes back to the beginning. 'I didn't know he felt this way.'

She has seen what I had seen as well. Lewis has drawn

his heart on the page. She shuts the book slowly. 'So where do you think they are?'

I shake my head, frowning. 'I don't know.'

Grace sighs and looks out my window to the dusky sky that always seems to have hints of rain in it. 'I've looked everywhere that I think Bonnie might be. Every place I can think of.' Her shoulders sag. I want to touch them. Instead, I say, 'I looked for Lewis at the pool. I saw them get the body and take it away.'

'That's when you thought it was Lewis.'

'They wouldn't tell me it wasn't.'

I see something pass over Grace's face. When she speaks, it's the softest she's ever spoken to me, ever spoken to anyone. 'That must have been terrible.'

I've seen terrible. I've seen my cousin dead on the ground. At least I knew Josh was dead. It was as certain as anything I've ever known. I remember the daymare I had at the pool again and for a second my throat closes over. I wait for it to relax before saying, 'It was. It was so terrible...'

The room is still and grey. Suddenly Grace stands up. 'Come on, Bull.'

I stand as well, knocking my guitar on its stand. It wobbles but I catch it before it goes over. 'What are we doing?'

'We're going to look for them.' She picks up the sketch-book but puts it down again. 'We don't need this anymore.'

I follow her out the door, wave to Ella who looks suspiciously at Grace then grins. I haven't got the energy to scowl at her but store it for later. We go out the front door and then Grace stops. 'Where are we going?' I ask her but she just shrugs. She seems so uncertain - so *un*Grace-like - that I make a decision. 'Let's start at school. We can work our way out from there.'

The light around us is that strange stormy yellow that you get when the sun slants through rain cloud. It bathes Grace and makes her seem unhealthy. I try not to look but walk beside her with my eyes on the footpath. She takes my hand, grabs it, and I close my fingers around hers just as tightly.

Our school is dark and unfriendly. Water has washed away the bark chip mulch from the garden beds and spread it out on the paths, staining them red. In the half-light, it's a bit like thick blood. We step through it and go towards our home room. The buildings are locked, and only one security light glows from the eave. I shake the door, look through the windows, check the roof. No one and nothing.

Grace pulls me away. Her fingers dig in to my palm but I don't mind. We have a tour of the school. In places, the rain has overflowed into classrooms and we can see where someone has stacked furniture high and mopped the floor. The gutter is off on the side near the library and hangs dangerously by a rivet or two. It starts to rain again as we walk, a light dusting of water that settles on Grace's hair like a thousand pieces of mirror before the yellow light fades away and the greyness of clouds settles around us.

We turn the corner and we're at the lockers. Alarm bells are ringing in my head. The lockers sit under a roof that is joined to the sports shed and I haven't been here for one year and four months. I see everything so clearly, even in the dullness. I see everyone from when Josh was here, milling around and shoving each other, and I see my locker next to his even though he was two years older. I see the way that our shoulders used to bang together as we went to get books out before school. I see his bag heaped on top of mine and kicked underneath and I can even smell mouldy sandwiches left in his locker but making mine seem to stink as well.

'Bull?' says Grace. 'What's the matter?'

I've let her go. My arms are folded over my chest. I've stopped out in the rain. I tear my eyes away from all those pictures in my head and look at Grace instead. She is staring at me intensely, studying me. I'd like to tell her what's happening. I try.

'I…'

There's nothing I can say to explain. It's my own nightmare.

'He's not here,' says Grace. She strides across to me, stands up on her tiptoes and kisses me.

Maybe it's the shock of her lips on mine, or maybe her words mean so much more to me than what she meant them to, but the pictures fade away and leave me alone. With Grace. Kissing Grace.

At last she pulls away, using her free hand to wipe the rain from my face. 'There's something about you, Bull,' she says carefully, as if she's made up her mind about something. 'Something I like.'

What could she possibly like about me? I don't say it but I think she guesses.

'It must be the way you think about things. The way you feel about things. Or maybe it's something to do with your music.'

I feel a bit like an insect, the way she's studying me. A large insect, maybe a really interesting large insect. But then I realize that in those times I've seen her watching me she wasn't just studying me, she was *seeing* me. Noticing me. I shake my head and tell her the truth. 'I don't play anymore.'

'*What?*'

She's so amazed that I blink.

'I don't play any music anymore.'

'Why not?'

'I can't.' She doesn't say anything. 'Just in case,' I explain.

'Okay,' she says slowly. 'You'd better start at the top with that one because it doesn't make any sense.'

Her dark eyes don't leave me alone. 'You said it yourself. That day in the music store. You said, *I think the music made them mad.*'

She frowns, trying to remember. Then she does. 'I wasn't talking about you.'

'No. You were talking about music. What it does to people.' My voice is getting louder. The rain gets heavier.

'Bull. What are you talking about?'

I'm drenched. The rain is running down the back of my neck. I feel stupid but I can't move. 'I don't want to be like Josh.'

The rain is so heavy it flattens Grace's curls. I can't believe her hair is so long. It stretches out down her arm until it nearly touches her elbow. She reaches up to push it out of her eyes. I see the old story of Josh pass over her face as she recalls that time, only last year, when he died and I was so out of it. Her gaze softens – well, I think it does. Maybe it's the water flooding her skin. She takes a step closer to me. 'Josh didn't play any music. Josh was loud and crazy even before anyone knew what was wrong with him. You're not like him at all.'

I shut my eyes, keeping them closed until her words flush right through me. *You're not like him.* I feel hope like a burning thing inside me. When I open my eyes she's very close to me and I hope that she'll kiss me again. She doesn't. Instead, she curls her hands over my arms and tugs them free of their knot. 'Come on, Bull. We aren't going to find them anywhere at school.'

We turn our backs on the cold grey lockers. Leaving them behind makes me realize that I don't ever have to think of them the same way again. Next time, the image to come into my head will be of Grace's kiss, not of a place Josh still haunts.

We walk through the rain until we're outside the schools gates. Grace's hand on my arm is warm. I glance down at it, see a blurred black dragon head. *You're not like him at all.* I smile, just a bit. 'Why do you do that?' I tap my finger on her hand.

She looks at it, lets my arm go, and splays her hand out in front of her. 'Good, isn't it? I like this one better.' She reefs her singlet top from her stomach. A perfect Celtic knot sits on her curved belly. 'Why do I do it? It's an experiment with body art. And it isn't permanent so I can change my mind. It *entertains* me.' She looks up at me. 'What do you think?'

She's grinning so much the rain is falling into her mouth. I put my arm out and wrap it around the bare skin of her back. I can hardly talk but I manage to say, 'I think it's great.'

'Thanks,' she says. 'So do I. I'm going to be a body artist one day. Maybe a tattooist. So I need to practise my designs. Do you want one?'

I think of her drawing something, anything, on my skin and nod.

'You need to think of a symbol. Something that means something to you. Otherwise it's just a picture that means nothing.'

I nod again, not able to think of anything symbolic at the moment. Except those lockers. Maybe the tree. Two things I don't want inked into my flesh. I don't want anything that reminds me of Josh on my body.

Then I remember the hut.

I come back to where we are, standing on the footpath wondering where Lewis and Bonnie could be.

The hut. The old bush hut out near the creek. Josh and I were the only ones who knew about it. Or were we? Josh and Bonnie were so close, he must have taken her there before.

'Grace,' I say, my voice rising into thunder. 'I know where they are.'

41

LEWIS

I have not eaten. There is no food. There will never be food again.

The water traps us. It's in my head. My brain is drowning.

She thinks I'm asleep. I'm not.

She thinks I'm mucking around. I'm not.

My lips are numb. My stomach pains. My body is dissolving.

She goes away.

She comes back crying. Bleeding. She stinks of mud and blood.

I see the walls turning blue grey to taupe. Frame by frame. Slow motion.

She shakes me. I hit her.

She goes away.

She comes back. Tips water in my mouth. It tastes like leaves. The river. Poison. I spit it out.

She talks. She doesn't make sense. She is an alien.

I feel her tug the bracelet from my arm.

I feel her roll me on my side. The ground is mud. Wet. Bad.

I feel her curl up behind me. She blends into me.

Then.

I don't feel anything.

I am a blank canvas.

42

BULL

'How far?' Grace gives me a worried look.

'I don't know. It's different going on foot. I'm usually on my bike.'

We walk fast but it takes a long time. At the edge of the park, I look out into the bush. I'm not really a *Lord of the Rings* fan, but the bush looks a lot like the forest near Helms Deep just before it ate the orcs. The trees are thick, and I can hear the creek winging itself away from the centre of town and ploughing down the hill.

'What now?'

I point to the track in front of us. 'There's an old house along there. Maybe they've got stuck on the other side of the creek.'

'How do you know about it?'

I think of Josh and me on that lonely track, and the crash of the bike as he pushed me over. 'Josh showed me. It was Josh's.'

'So Bonnie would have known about it as well. That makes sense.'

'I should have thought of it earlier.'

Grace shrugs. 'You've thought of it now. How do we get there?'

We stand at the edge of the trees with the rain falling harder and the air getting so much darker as dusk and more storms approach. I think about going home to get a torch but that seems like a waste of time. Silently, I start forward and Grace is by my side.

The trees are wet and hang over the road so that every now and then they slap me in the face. I can't remember seeing all the little tracks leading off into the bush before but I ignore them, concentrating on the creek. I remember the creek, how I rode through the tiny patch of water that it was then while Josh leapt it like a hurdler. I remember hoping that I wouldn't get a puncture on the jagged creek rocks because I knew that Josh wouldn't help me and I'd have to carry my bike home over my shoulder. I remember that we made it safely through and it wasn't long after that Josh pointed into the bush and I saw the shape of something man-made and old. It was the hut. It was so ancient that it had turned the colours of the bush, rusty red and brown.

'Bull?' Grace says. 'It's getting pretty dark.'

The sound of the creek nearly drowns her voice out even though we can't see it yet. 'Yeah,' I say loudly. 'I don't think it's much further.'

She starts jogging and I run hard to keep up. Grace runs without any effort and I can't help watching her silhouette in the dimness, her strong legs powering her forward. It gets darker still but the rain eases up, helping the situation a bit. We go around a bend and the creek comes into view. We stop at its edge.

This is no creek. This is a raging river. It's white capped, glittering in the patches of sky light that are beginning to appear as clouds move away. It hurls itself through the bush, leaving its bed and making new pathways on either side. Young trees bend over in its grip. Dark things are caught in it and rush past us. Are they bodies?

Grace steps as close as she can to the torrent of water. 'What do we do now?'

I look past the creek, up the road, into the bush. It's too dark to see anything. 'Lewis!' I yell. 'Lew!' My voice is useless against the creek noise.

'Bonnie!' Grace yells too. Her voice seems to rise above the noise. She sounds a bit like a cockatoo.

'Keep shouting, Grace.' I leave her and go up the creek a little way, looking for some way of getting across. I almost stumble over it before I see it – a large tree down, its roots in the air. It spans the creek but how far I can't really tell. Most of it, maybe? Enough to jump the rest of the way? I go back to Grace.

'I'm going to try to get across. There's a tree I can use as a bridge.'

Grace looks up at me. Her face is a ghostly white. 'I don't think you should. What if it gives way? Face it, Bull. You're pretty heavy. Maybe I should go across. Maybe we should call the police.'

'You don't know where the hut is so you can't go.' I'm not one hundred per cent sure where it is either but I have a better idea than Grace. Every second we wait, though, is another second of darkness. 'I'll crawl across the tree. At least I'm too heavy to knock off if something comes down the creek.' I pat the pocket with my phone. 'I'll text you if I find anything and you can call the police.'

She lets her arms drop. 'This is crazy.'

I look back at the raging creek. 'Yeah, it is.' I step away from her and head towards the tree.

This time I do hit it before I see it. It's dark enough that everything has blended into everything else. I grope my way to the very edge of the water, keeping my hands on the trunk, and pull myself up until I'm on my hands and knees facing the fallen tree top. I start to crawl.

The noise is loudest half way along and I can't hear anything else but the boiling, angry water. I know that my heart is thudding hard because I can feel it. I can't see the roots of the tree behind me and I can't see the top of the tree in front. I can just see my hands on the bark and those little white splashes of water that are trying to leap up and get me. I definitely can't see Grace or Bonnie or Lewis.

Then my hands tangle in little twigs and I've reached the end of my bridge. I pause, wondering what to do. The tree has sloped downwards as it got skinnier and now I can feel the water tugging at the tree trunk, making it bob up and down. My weight sinks it lower into the water. I can't see the other side of the creek but maybe I'm almost there. I look back in Grace's direction but, of course, can't see a thing. I have two choices - go back, jump forward.

I'm wobbling on my hands and knees trying not to do the wrong thing when Josh leaps into my mind. It's as if he's been waiting until I could do absolutely nothing about it. I see him in front of me, on the track to the old hut, running hard. His eyes are wild but he's grinning as he goes. He's faster than I am on my bike and draws ahead. I follow him, like I always do.

'That's my secret hideaway,' he yells pointing into the bush. 'No one knows I go there. It's mine.' We go along the track for about twenty metres then he stops. I nearly run into the back of him and brake hard, spinning the back wheel out. He leaps at me and the bike crashes over as he lands on top. I'm not as big then as I am now so his weight plus the bike crushes my pelvis into the dirt. 'You don't know about this place,' he says into my face, putting his hand against my cheek and pinning me to the ground. 'Do you, Bull?'

I can just get my mouth open. 'What place?' I say, and I've given the only correct answer there was. Josh laughs and jumps off me, running ahead along the track like demons are after him. I get up shakily, brush the silty dirt from my head and hip and get back on my bike.

I'm on the tree trunk again but I've stood up. The tree bobs. I leap into the dark, jumping like once Josh had jumped the baby creek, and land in water up to my thighs. The unexpected ground force sends shock waves right through my body and into my head but I scramble forward, plough through the water, slip once so I go under, pull myself up and out. 'I made it!' I yell to the invisible Grace. There's no reply that I can hear. I stare hard at the ground in front of me and follow what I think is the shape of the track.

How am I ever going to find the old hut? I pull my phone out, hope it hasn't died from my creek crossing, try the light. It's fine. I shine light into the trees. It's not much help. I go up the track as far as I think I should then take off into the bush, using my hands to feel the way. Twice I fall over things I don't even see. The first time, a stick gouges my leg painfully and I feel blood run into my sock. The second time I hit my head on a rock and the sky spins for a moment. I get up wobbly, but the clouds roll past again and let light in. I get a glimpse of a solid colour, black in the dark. The wall of the hut. I am here.

I stumble through the doorway and go down on my hands and knees again just like I had on the tree bridge.

'Bull!'

It's Bonnie. Some starlight comes through the hole in the roof. I crawl towards her.

'I tried to get back across the creek. I tried!'

She's sitting on some logs crying and bleeding from cuts to her legs. There's a dark shape across her. I feel the shape and it's Lewis with his head on her lap. He is not moving.

'No, Lew. Come on, don't do this.' I shake him and his eyes flicker open. They shine for a moment and then he's away again.

I put my forehead down on his.

Catch me, Bull!

I sit up and seize his shoulders. 'Come on. Wake up.'

He swipes at me but his aim is bad. 'What?' he manages in a voice that fades. 'Wha?'

'Lew, you have to hang on. Keep with it, hang in there.'

His eyes roll around, I can see them moving under his lids. Once or twice he nearly gets them open so I shake him hard and sharp until he does. 'Don't. Donnnd.'

'See?' I say to him loudly. 'You are sick. I told you. You are a sick prick. You should have listened to me, I knew what I was saying.' I yell into his face. 'I said you were sick and I was right!'

That's when he struggles upright, nearly making it to sitting.

Bonnie kneels behind him. 'What are you doing, Bull? Leave him alone.' Her face is soggy with tears.

'You are really sick, you idiot.' I still have Lewis's shoulders so I pull him close to me. 'You can't say you're not because here you are, looking like a heap of shit.'

It's hard to see but I think tears are running down his cheeks. His breathing is fast and I can smell the sweetness of his sickness through the rot stink of the hut. I don't want to do it anymore but I think it's helping. 'You are as sick as a dying dog!'

He vomits suddenly, all over me. It's warm and watery.

I can feel it through my shirt. I don't let him go, not even to wipe his mouth.

Bonnie is crying. She reaches around for me. 'You're a bastard, Bull!'

I let her claw me but I'm not letting him go. Lewis's eyes are fixed on me now. They're open. I hold him. We just stare at each other, me covered in his slime and his acidy breath. It's a long stare and I blink first. I think I see his lips curve into a brief smile.

'Bull, Bull, Bull.'

His eyes close. I shake him awake. They crank open.

'I sick.' He gives the faintest of nods. 'I sick. You not.'

I put my forehead back on his. Yeah, so I'm crying now. 'No, mate.' I shake him again. Our heads bang. 'I'm not.'

He shakes his head slowly, slower, stops.

'Come on, Lewis.' Come on, Josh.

Catch me.

THE NEXT PART IS SIMPLE.

I text Grace.

She calls for help.

The police come.

Lights appear.

Men in orange overalls swing through the door.

There are quick, low voices that tell me by their tone how much of an emergency this is. Lewis has a drip stabbed into him, gets strapped to a stretcher and is taken away, first by ambulance and then by helicopter.

Bonnie and I go back across the creek on improvised rope swings.

Grace hugs me.

Grace hugs Bonnie who collapses.

Lewis goes into intensive care in the city three hours' drive away and they hope they're in time to save him.

So simple.

WHEN I WAS as low as I could go last year, Lewis came over to my place and gave me a CD. He'd burnt it himself and labelled it and written out its entire contents. There was a sketch of him on the disc. I was in bed, that place where I'd spent so much time over the months since Josh died. I usually went straight from school to bed. My room smelt stale from me breathing through unbrushed teeth. The winter fan swished it slowly around.

'Listen,' Lewis said, 'this is my top 100. Stuff what those *radio* stations say is the top 100. How do they know that the same people aren't voting again and again for their favourite songs? It's taken me fourteen hours and twenty minutes to get this together.' Lewis opened my CD player and put it in. 'At 100,' he announced dramatically, 'it's The Uglymen with *Uproar*.'

We listened to that song and then the next. Five songs later, he was still sitting on my bed, not talking but drawing something in that mini-sketchbook he used to carry in his pocket. Another three songs and I said, 'What's your number one?'

'You'll have to wait.' Lewis reached over and put the CD case on my desk. 'Or you could read that and find out.' He kept drawing. I kept listening. Another six songs. I got out of bed, feeling shaky, and got the case. I couldn't read it until I was safely back in bed. When I saw his first choice, I said, 'You've got to be joking.'

Lewis shook his head. 'No, it's true.'

'Skinny Healey's "Mister Sometimes"?'

'There's no one that plays trumpet like Skinny.'

Well, I couldn't argue with that.

Another three songs played.

'I'd have a different number one.'

At this, Lewis stood up. 'I know,' he said, putting his sketchbook away in his back pocket. 'That's your challenge. You do your top 100.' He opened the door to go. 'See you later.'

I must have played that CD thirty times in a row, looping it over and over, day and night. It took me forty-five hours and thirty-seven minutes to make my own CD, and that was over six whole weeks. When I finished, I walked over to Lewis's place.

'Bull,' Lewis said after I'd bashed on his bedroom window, 'it's two o'clock in the morning.'

'Finished,' I said, posting the CD through the hole in the fly wire screen.

As I walked away, I heard him say, 'You've got to be joking. You put *Chopin* at number one?'

It's whatever gets you through.

I TELL Grace what it was like in the short, horrible time in the hut. She listens, drawing on my arm in thick black pen as I sit on my bed.

'You know, in the dark, he could have been Josh.' I breathe in and breathe out. 'He could have been dead. Lewis might have been dead.'

Grace keeps drawing, her hand steady and slow.

'He might still die.'

Grace keeps drawing as I cry, she doesn't even pause. But when she's finished and I'm not, she holds me, her arms gripping my back. I cry about everything. Josh. Me. Lew. The terrible things we inherit and the terrible things that just happen.

The études we play.

She keeps hold.

43

LEWIS

My head clears enough to handle the bright lights of intensive care and I see that Mum has never left the chair beside the bed. I make out other shapes, too. Nurses with unfamiliar faces and Dr Nightingale in deep conversation with another doctor-shape. I even see Sam Keally drawing something in a black sketchbook. No, not Sam Keally, just my care nurse writing something down. I chuckle. Sam Keally in a hospital? At least I'd get to see him then. I laugh harder.

'Lewis?'

Mum is hovering over me, a smile on her pale face.

'Hey, Mum.'

She pats my hand, carefully avoiding needle sites.

'All good?' I say.

She doesn't hesitate. 'All good.'

I'm pretty tired so I let myself drift in and out until Mum puts something on my bed.

'What's that?'

'It's from William Healey. He sent it in with your Dad.'

'Dad's here?'

'Here I am.' Dad is at the foot of the bed. He grips my ankle as if he's not letting go. I have so much to say to him but not now, not here.

Instead, I pick up Bull's parcel. It's his music player, the green one with the deep scratch on the back. I turn it on. There's a playlist marked 'Lew.' It has one song on it, untitled. I put the earbuds in with shaking hands.

The song plays.

It's terrible.

Bull can't sing and the piano doesn't substitute for a trumpet. It's the worst rendition of *Mister Sometimes* I've ever heard.

I love it.

44

BULL

When Grace leaves, I look for the first time at what she's drawn on my arm. It's a bass clef on a stave, a strong square symbol stamped on my left triceps like a sailor's anchor. I study it in the mirror attached to my wardrobe and see that she's signed it with a G that curls over like a reversed question mark.

My phone zings a message. It's Grace.

Well? she texts.

Exactly right, I text.

I put the phone down and go out to Great-Grandma Broadbent's piano. Ella is on the couch. She doesn't say anything as I flip the lid up. I run my fingers over the worn ivory and ebony keys. Then I play my number one, right through, easily, as if I'd never stopped practising.

Music pulses through my blood.

ACKNOWLEDGMENTS

This novel was written as part of my PhD from the University of Canberra. Thanks to Anthony Eaton, supervisor extraordinaire, and others that helped along their way with comments, advice, and excellent humour.

ABOUT THE AUTHOR

P. J. Harvey lives in Victoria, Australia, with her family. She writes junior and young adult fiction under the names of Pam Harvey and P. J. Harvey, and has published over twenty books for children. She was the recipient of a May Gibbs Creative Fellowship in 2014.

www.pamjharvey.com